D1824515

In memory of my parents, Robert and Margaret. Their energy for living and courage for loving continue to inspire me.

Contents

FOREWORD

In October 2023, Miriam and I met for the first time in Landshut. It was a truly special moment: historian Matthias Weniger from the Bavarian National Museum in Munich returned to Miriam a precious heirloom that the Nazis had stolen from her ancestors in 1939 – a beautiful silver bowl that once belonged to her great-grandparents, Cäcilie and Adolf Hirsch, who had lived in Landshut since 1897. Miriam immediately entrusted the bowl to me, allowing me to include it in the exhibition I was curating on National Socialism in Landshut. This bowl became the centrepiece of the exhibition.

I often shared its tragic story with visitors – the story of Miriam's family's persecution during the Nazi era and how, thanks to Miriam's generosity, the bowl found its way back to Landshut. Since 2023, this bowl has symbolised a unique connection between Miriam and me. I felt incredibly fortunate to see her again in the summer of 2024, when I had the pleasure of showing her and her husband the entire exhibition.

Now, writing these words for the publication of her family's memoir is a profound honour for me. I greatly admire how Miriam approaches her family's history – with such warmth, sincerity and authenticity. I hope that, through writing this book, she has found what she was searching for: a deeper sense of identity. Landshut is, and always will be, an important part of that.

Dr Doris Danzer, historian and curator of the Landshut museum
www.doris-danzer.de
www.museen-landshut.de

FOREWORD: FROM MUNICH TO ORKNEY

With this book, a self-proclaimed treasure hoarder has become a sharer of treasures. In many of the families I deal with when returning silver items stolen from their ancestors in 1939, one person keeps the stories. However, very few of these story keepers ever dare to make the step of opening their findings to the public. This courage and immense effort cannot be underestimated. The Nazis not only succeeded in achieving their goal of eradicating (almost) all European Jews. They also came very close to obliterating almost every memory of them. One of the most chilling aspects of Miriam Landor's account is the fact that, when she first read Lilli Palmer's story about Cilly Hirsch's sad end, she was not even aware that Cilly had been her great grandmother. Another is that she came to know many family details at a late stage, often from strangers or even foreigners. In parallel, when my predecessor published a catalogue of the museum's silver objects of Jewish origin in 2019, he noted on Adolf Hirsch: "No biographical data known". Adolf Hirsch, once one of the most powerful merchants of Landshut, had been almost totally forgotten. In our case, as in Miriam's, the work of the Landshut *Stolperstein* team was decisive to save him from total oblivion.

It makes hard reading that Cilly had been able to visit her exiled family in London – and returned to her death in Germany. Sadly, among the families I am in touch with, this story is not at all unique. The same holds true for the observation that the survivors and their children rarely spoke about what they had experienced and witnessed. And many survivor families describe to me what it means to have grown up without grandparents. The fact that the descendants have lost touch with the German language and are unable to read the last letters of their ancestors makes this silence and absence even more palpable.

Deep traumata not only haunted the first and second generations, but continue to haunt the third and fourth. Of course they are not least a consequence of that silence, and of these absences. Tragically, it appears the grandchildren of the victims still suffer much more than the descendants of the perpetrators and the henchmen. The account Miriam Landor gives of these traumata and of the voids that can never be closed again is particularly vivid, detailed – and blunt. In addition, her own professional background and experience as a psychologist makes this approach yet more valuable, deeper and convincing – and all the more frightening.

It is moving as well as shaming for German readers to observe how benignly the author treats the country that had served her grandparents and great grandparents so badly. This amazing longing for understanding might be a necessary tool if one is struggling for redemption from the evils of the past. Again, the author's wish to understand seems to go much deeper than what we sadly observe in too many descendants of the erstwhile offenders. The book contains many graphic details – yet is still very benevolent. Many more sad stories could have been added – for example that, in his last months in Landshut, Adolf Hirsch would have needed a special permit to visit the grave of his son Erich and that of his wife Cilly, in the New Israelite Cemetery in Munich. After April 1942, Jews were barred from using public transport, and there are 70 kilometres between Landshut and Munich. But at least Cilly got a grave. Adolf's name is listed on the headstone as well – but, his grave is, as Paul Celan put it so poignantly, in the airs.

Today we are living again in an era in which racial hatred, blatant force and violence seem to get the upper hand over compassion, affection and righteousness. And in which many people, not just in Germany, think enough has been said about the Holocaust, and we should just turn the page and move on. This book shows that it is worth fighting against the oblivion, and that the wounds are open still, more so than ever. Miriam's entire account underlines that we can only master the future if we face up to the past. Might this call from the edges of Europe contribute to making this continent a slightly better place?

Dr Matthias Weniger, curator and head of provenance research
Bayerisches Nationalmuseum

INTRODUCTION

This is the story of how I came to uncover what happened to my father's family. *Stumbling Stones: The Holocaust, my family and me* follows my quest to understand their painful history, and its impact on my life.

The Landauers were assimilated Jews who fled Germany for London in 1938, when the Nazis stripped my grandfather, Dr Richard Landauer, of his successful art book publishing business in Munich. Some died, some disappeared, some were broken – and some developed extraordinary resilience.

Stolpersteine are inscribed brass plaques, "stumbling stones" to make a passer-by pause and reflect. They memorialise former victims of Nazism; there are seven *Stolpersteine* in Landshut for members of my family. And I have a "stumbling stone" in my own life – a sense of being a rootless outsider, stemming from a disrupted childhood following my father's postings around the world for the United Nations Development Programme.

I learn about other family members who were part of the diaspora: Fritz Landauer, the well-known architect of the Augsburg synagogue, made a new reputation in London; Walter Landauer, brand designer and founder of the internationally famous firm, Landor Associates, studied in London then settled in San Francisco; Lilli Palmer, Hollywood star, artist and author, left Berlin to forge her career across Europe and America.

During visits to Bavaria, where the Landauer family came from, I meet with kindness and honesty from those Germans concerned to address their country's past. With their help, and through letters and photographs, artefacts and documents, I learn about the impact of persecution and exile on my family, and the tragic fates of those who stayed behind. I have named those in official positions who helped me, as their identities are a matter of public record. To those whom I met in a private capacity, I gave the choice of using their real names or a pseudonym. They have all read the parts of the book that relate to them. To preserve their right to privacy, I have kept descriptions of these people and their homes to a minimum.

My career in developmental psychology underpins my reflections on human experience, and on events in my own life. Discovering who my family were brings about a change in my understanding of how the past has shaped me.

Why was it important to write this book? Genocides are still occurring throughout the world, sending refugees to flee with what few possessions they can preserve. The second and third generations of any survivors have inherited trauma, grief and a loss of home culture; the links to the past have been broken and their sense of identity and belonging are fragmented. Maybe you share this experience, or know someone in your community who does. We are one world. Understanding ourselves and each other, past events and future possibilities, is the only way forward.

Family Trees

Landauer Family Tree

Richard Landauer	Edith Hirsch
1882 - 1960	1900 - 1942

Eva Maria Landauer
1922 - 1988

Stefan Klaus Landauer
1925 - 2013

Robert Felix Landauer
1927 - 1986
My father

Kirkland Family Tree

Frederick Thomas Kirkland
1895 - 1984

Mabel Tarlton
1894 - 1984

Margaret Kirkland
1928 - 2000
My mother

Landor Family Tree

Robert Felix Landor
1927 - 1986

Margaret Kirkland
1928 - 2000

Mark Christian Landor
1950 -

Miriam Sharon Landor
1953 -
Author

Renate Felicia Landor
1962 -

1

SWITZERLAND, JANUARY 2014

The shift in my understanding starts at a small dinner party in Switzerland. Our host tells us about her other dinner guest, a German visitor. Her old friend Hans, she says, is the widower of a much-loved teaching colleague, and he comes to see her from time to time; he's just changing his clothes after a day's ramble around Alpine peaks. We watch a tall, solidly built man come down the stairs at the edge of the dining space, treading carefully on each open step. This man is about to change my perception of myself, my family and the Holocaust, for ever.

I make my usual overture whenever I meet someone from Germany:

'I'm actually half German – my father's family left Germany just in time, just before the war broke out. They went to London and settled there.'

Hans has a sensitive way of attuning himself to those around him.

'Really?' His face comes alive with interest. 'Do you know why they left?'

'Yes,' I reply. 'They were Jewish – racially though not by religion.' For some reason, I always think this is an important point to make, although I never stop to reflect why.

'So, they had to leave?'

'Yes.'

'And are there *Stolpersteine* with their names?'

'Are there ... what?'

I have never heard of *Stolpersteine*.

Hans explains that *Stolpersteine* can be translated as 'stumbling stones'. Each one looks like a brass cobblestone, engraved with the name,

9

date and fate of a victim of National Socialism. These are set into the pavement outside their last home. So many more than the six million Jews were persecuted, he reminds us – gypsies, communists, political dissenters, homosexuals, 'degenerate' artists ... The idea is that passers-by will stumble in their thoughts, as they recognise that an otherwise forgotten person, forced to flee or murdered by the Nazis, had existed in this place. We pause a moment to reflect on this sobering image, imagining bright gleams snagging people's attention as they hurry through grey streets, then the conversation flows on. We take turns to dip and swirl our long forks in the fondue, savouring the sharp scent of cheese, wine and garlic.

As the dinner party ends, we go out into the dark winter night. Our host's outdoor light has failed, she explains, and the blackness seems palpable. Soft snowflakes kiss our cheeks and melt to nothing in an instant. We stand still for a moment after the front door closes, waiting for our night vision to kick in before making for our cars. I can hear by his voice that Hans is turning to me.

'Tell me where your father's family lived. I can make enquiries for you, find out if you could get a stumbling stone made for your father, if you would like?'

I thank him, feeling moved by his offer, and we exchange correspondence details.

As I lie in bed that night, thinking over the surprising outcome of the evening, the term 'stumbling stone' takes on a deeper, more personal meaning. It seems to summarise what life has done to us, the barrier to our wellbeing caused by people or events. My own stumbling stone, I muse, is my feeling of being unanchored, of not being sure what or where my roots are, and who I am. My expat childhood is like a hollow chasm underlying the carefully packed earth I have laid down throughout my adult years; at any moment my toe could catch in a crack, sending me tumbling down.

At this point I know very little about my father Robert's early life. I know that he was the youngest of three children, that his father, Richard, was much older than Edith, his mother, and that Edith had died when Robert was still a child; I know that they had been forced to leave Germany on the eve of the Second World War, and that my grandfather had eventually returned to Bavaria as a widower.

I don't pause to wonder why Richard went back, having been ejected from his homeland so traumatically. On the contrary, the fact he returned to Germany fitted in with my idle notion of 'that was then; this is a new now'. I don't stop to wonder how few years – not even two decades – had passed between Richard's enforced leaving and his repatriation. That time span was a short fraction of Richard's life. The Holocaust was not 'history' for him, as it was for me.

When I was quite young, perhaps four or five years old, and living in Nairobi, my brother Mark and I had Saturday lessons with a German woman so that we could, with help, write to Grandfather in his own language. My next memory of connecting with him was our visit to him in Feldafing, Bavaria, when I was six. And finally, when the film Cabaret came out in 1972, I felt a special connection. The smash-hit musical was based on Christopher Isherwood's semi-autobiographical story set in Berlin in the early 1930s, with the contrasting hedonism and growing Nazi brutality of the Weimar Republic's final years. My mother told me that my great-grandparents had owned a department store, just like the character Natalia Landauer in the film, and that my dad's family name had also been Landauer, before they anglicised it to Landor. She said that, as Jews, they had suffered similar persecution, but she gave me no details.

My father never spoke of his early life, except for a few anecdotes. He used to tell us children about a time when his family combed the neighbourhood for him, their lost youngest son. They eventually found him curled up behind the long, blue velvet drapes in their Munich drawing room, where he had fallen asleep during a game of hide-and-seek.

What else did I know of my German family? When I was six, we lived in London briefly, between stints in Kenya and Ghana. My father took us to meet three elderly relatives. One of them was called Aunt Liesel, whom we thought of as Aunt Measles. We knew the word 'measles', but Liesel – what sort of name was that?

'*Komm her*, see vat I haff for you!'

Their German accents were almost impenetrable, and their enthusiasm over Mark and me, their offerings of a strange-looking toy truck, some crayons and unfamiliar baked cheesecake, rendered us catatonic with shyness.

Otherwise, there were only my unmarried Aunt Eva, with whom we were living, and my Uncle Stephen, his English wife Phyllis, and their children, Karen and Francis. Aunt Eva made a chocolate hedgehog cake for any child's birthday, following a recipe remembered from her German youth. Slivers of almonds, the hedgehog's spines, covered the brown chocolate frosting.

'Go on, it's your birthday – have another slice.'

I did so and promptly threw up. Either my stomach was unaccustomed to the cake's richness or Eva's liberal use of margarine was too much for me. I could never resist her hedgehog cakes but was always sick afterwards. I don't enjoy margarine to this day.

Underpinning my reminiscence of these members of my father's family were a few precious artefacts, somehow preserved from their cultured life in their Munich apartment. Because of my career in psychology, I now understand the significance of these objects. A person's identity, their sense of belonging, is rooted firmly in their home and their possessions. In this space and surrounded by these familiar objects, a person should be able to feel safe. If, on the other hand, home is a place of internal threats, belongings can become imbued with fear, triggering flashbacks. Our possessions refer us back to that sense of who we are – a person of worth or a victim of others. The term 'object of reference' also alludes to a communication system in special education, which gives a concrete shape to an abstract future event. For example, presenting a spoon can prepare a non-verbal person to expect a meal, or offering both a shaker and a woolly hat can invite them to choose between playing with musical instruments or being taken outside. For a refugee, objects can take on a great significance; they refer backwards, to a time and a place of security and comfort, the home they had to leave. Such belongings become imbued with a special respect and sentiment.

The few treasures the Landauers had preserved must have reminded them of their previous happy years in Munich, before the Nazis took so much from them. As a child I was particularly intrigued by our stately German eight-day mantelpiece clock, with its Roman numerals etched into the brass face and its hourly striking. It is housed in a polished dark wooden case, with glass sides and doors, rising to a dignified portico above. My parents forbade me to touch it. One empty Sunday morning, however, I decided to take my turn to wind it. I had finished my book, the weather was too bad to go out and there was 'nothing to do' – my perpetual complaint in childhood. Standing gingerly on a chair, I carefully, so carefully, tried to copy exactly what I saw my mother do every week. I was just being helpful, I told myself. There were three keyholes, and I wound each one. Just like in a Grimms' fairy tale, the clock began to strike and didn't stop at twelve. It didn't stop at all. Crying hysterically, I ran to find my mother. The clock went on striking until it had completely wound down. Apparently, my parents never wound up the quarter-hour striking mechanism, from the third keyhole, because something was wrong with it. Seeing my genuine terror, my mother said my disobedience had been punished enough. The clock has now fallen to me as part of my inheritance, but I am reluctant to wind it up and set it going.

We also had the oil painting of Aunt Eva as a baby, with impossibly round, black eyes that follow you around the room. My mother whitewashed the iron relief of Great-Grandfather Sigmund's bust in a criminal act of 1960s upcycling – it was too gloomy, she said. We used the Landauer engraved silver serviette rings throughout my childhood – heavy oblongs of solid silver, with lines of silver beading top and bottom and each person's initials etched onto the side – but kept my grandmother Edith's trousseau of monogrammed linen carefully stored away.

Sigmund Landauer 9.4.1916

When I visited the Jewish Museum in Berlin, I was entranced to find an entire room of family possessions that refugees had preserved in their flight from persecution; I could recognise the blue-flowered Rosenthal china dinner service, the silver cruet set and the cream lace tablecloth, as we have them all too. These carefully preserved objects formed a revered reminder of who they really were.

Through some strange displacement, it was my English mother, Margaret, a Landauer by marriage alone, who became the keeper of her husband's family history and possessions. Having grown up in Ashbourne in the English Midlands, I think she must have found Robert's background far more romantic and interesting than her own. The Landauers had been well off, and their lives had centred around art, music and literature, first in Munich and then in London; this was so different from the Kirklands' background of carefully making ends meet in a provincial market town.

My mother tried to interest me in the photo album of my father's childhood, in which she meticulously labelled the monochrome images from a vanished era. (It is interesting that she made no such album of her own family.) But I was at a time in my life when I was looking forward, not back, and missed the opportunity to learn more. Our third child was a baby of only a few months when my father died, and I was busy with my toddlers, and my grief.

After my mother's death, I inherited many of the Landauer treasures that she preserved so carefully. In my turn, I have become the keeper of our German family's belongings. I think she valued these artefacts because she romanticised the wealth and culture they denoted, whereas for me, their presence gives me a feeling of identity, following my rootless childhood. Like a dragon, 'precious' was the word I used to defend them against my family's own need for more space as they grew up. I have turned from a keeper into a hoarder.

It occurs to me now that, like my mother, I find my father's family background fascinating and romantic. The women of our family I perhaps take for granted; they feel known, part of me, as in my childhood I lived from time to time in Ashbourne among my mother's family. So, as I approach old age, I am trying to puzzle this out. I want to explore my identity through my own life experiences, and through my father's life and his relationships with my mother, with his siblings and with his father.

To work out who I am, I need to know where I came from.

Hans' simple offer to explore 'stumbling stones' on my behalf was to become a strengthening beam of light, illuminating my father's family and history, and deepening my understanding of myself.

2

THE ORKNEY ISLANDS, SCOTLAND, 1991

Sparrows squabbled at the bird feeder. It was rare to have such a calm summer day. I glanced up to look over the flat waters of Kirkwall Bay; no white horses pranced across the sea to the low-lying island of Shapinsay that day. In this stillness, the scents of honeysuckle and wild rose overlaid fresh-cut grass as my mower striped the lawn. An unfamiliar car swerved into our drive and came to an abrupt halt. A woman rushed towards me, her body leaning forward in urgent emotion.

'How can you bear to speak to me?' she said, voice intense, head jutting towards me.

I recognised the German mother of my most recent client, an endearing little boy with bright blue eyes and a glorious blonde quiff. Freddy had just been referred to me in my role as support teacher for children with special needs.

'I'm sorry?' I could feel my instinctive smile of welcome battling with a frown of incomprehension as I stopped the lawnmower.

'How can you be in the same room as me? How can you even touch my child?' Her tone was anguished and her hands fluttered in distress.

'I don't know what you mean? Freddy is absolutely lovely. I'm very happy to work with you, find out what we can do to help him learn ... '

'But your father ... '

Then I started to understand.

'Berit, it was so long ago. We're a different generation,' I began. 'We can't live our lives based on what our grandparents did.'

As I do whenever I meet someone from Germany, I had told her I was half German, that my father's family had fled when he was a child, arriving in London just before war broke out. Instead of welcoming me as a fellow national, as I hoped, I found they sometimes turned away, looked embarrassed and changed the subject. But no one had ever responded like Berit, with this strange, delayed reaction. At the time of our first meeting, we had focused all our attention on Freddy.

In my experience, parents of children with special needs sometimes feel immense guilt, even though they know there is no rational reason to do so. I've also learnt that German children of the post-war generation were taught at school to be ashamed of their country's crimes during the Second World War, and of the complicity, if not active involvement, of their parents and grandparents, relatives and neighbours. Perhaps, I realised, these negative emotions, guilt and shame, were compounding each other for Berit.

We stood awkwardly at the edge of the lawn. I didn't want to invite her into the house where my own children were enjoying their Saturday morning of play; this problem needed to be sorted out between us first.

I leant forward to touch her arm and said,

'Here we both are, making new lives for ourselves in Orkney – we've been welcomed and made part of the Orkney community. That's because we're needed to join in with our families, and to contribute whatever skills we have. And where we came from, and what happened fifty years ago before we were even born, that isn't important at all. You've got a gorgeous child who needs a bit of extra help just now, and I've got the best job in the world, supporting families where I can. And that's all we need to think about.'

Eventually I managed to convince her that she held no blame in my mind for what had happened to my father's family in Nazi Germany. She went home, reassured, and I returned to cutting the grass. At that time in my life, half a century after my great-grandparents died in the

Holocaust and twenty years before I learned about it, I really believed that the events of my parents' early lives were history.

We had covered the Second World War in history lessons at school. We learnt all about its roots, its key events, its outcome. My claim of being half German wasn't even completely accurate, I suspected; my father, Robert, and his siblings, Eva and Stefan, had all been nationalised as British subjects when they were young adults, and certainly thought of themselves as English.

But me – who am I? After a disrupted childhood, attending ten schools in eighteen years as my family followed my father's international career, I am repeating his experience of being a stranger in a new culture: one who doesn't belong and must strive to fit in.

Looking back on the incident a few decades later, I realise I didn't really reflect on the significance of that strange episode. It stuck in my memory, of course, but at that time I was busy all my waking hours, dividing my time between caring for my family, studying for further qualifications when the children were asleep, and getting to grips with an absorbing new job. My husband, J, also had a responsible post in the local authority. His extensive range of interests outside his job were our children, the garden, art and nature. We both filled every moment. On the rare occasions we went out alone together, we talked about the practical demands of family life, celebrated achievements and puzzled over difficulties, but without making time to delve deeply into much else.

I am thinking myself back into that time. Our first child James was an inventor. He made worlds from sticks and stones; yachts from driftwood, nails and string; racing games from computer code. Eric, our second child was an engineer. He constructed an igloo by hollowing out a giant snowball; made working engines from Lego Technic; composed tunes on his fiddle. And Naomi, our youngest – a designer – drew colourful place settings for everyone; made over her room endlessly; chose her own outfits and prepared her own packed lunches. Siblings often choose different spheres to make their own, whilst sharing their play and competing with each other.

Their childhoods were so different to my own that it didn't occur to me to try to show them my past, to talk about my own time of growing up. A fragmented childhood spent in Africa and the Americas, educated in local schools and boarding schools, had no points of reference to the childhoods J and I were giving our three children. I thought the best way to deal with my own rootlessness was to give the next generation a fixed and stable community to grow up in. Chronic anxiety led me to try too hard in every area of my life: I worked hours of overtime, completing the paperwork in the early hours before the family woke, and studying for extra qualifications through the Open University. I read tomes and took courses in parenting skills. I worried endlessly about how best to help our children fit in. I was engrossed in the present and absorbed in helping us move towards our future. The past was a place of disruption, of constantly moving on. My now, not my then, was what I was focusing on, to find some sense of belonging for my family.

And now I think about it, perhaps that was part of the reason for my father's silence about his childhood, uprooted from Munich to Landshut to London. Was it just too different to the one he gave us, his children, to make bridging the gap possible?

Nothing changed over the next decade. I didn't think any more about my father's family history. I stayed busy in the same way, bringing up our three children, maintaining a marriage, household and friendships, establishing and furthering my career. Sometimes I toyed with the idea of finding a therapist to help me explore who I was, and how my peripatetic childhood had affected my adult life, but there never seemed to be sufficient time, money or urgency.

One day though, in the year before our youngest child prepared to leave home for university, I drove straight through a stop junction. Fortunately, the oncoming car on the main road took evasive action and gave a loud blast on the horn. There was no collision, but it was a wake-up call for me. I drove home shakily, and very carefully, and phoned our medical practice for an appointment. I told our GP what had happened, explaining that my loss of concentration had been due to a long spell of poor sleep, and asked for help with my insomnia.

He considered me thoughtfully.

'Or perhaps you could be depressed? That's how your manner seems to me ... Here's a prescription to help you sleep, for the next few days. Think over what I said and come back and see me next week.'

At first I rejected the very idea, but I did some research into symptoms: low mood, catastrophising, black-and-white thinking, low energy, poor sleep ... I finally recognised that the pressure I put myself under to help others professionally, and my lifelong lack of self-care, had indeed led to a major depression. In fact, I had suffered from bouts of low mood at boarding school, where my daily private journal entry usually began 'Felt depressed ... '. Perhaps there had been more to it than adolescence, or plain homesickness. I vowed to look after myself better, and over the next decade I learnt to recognise warning signs and take action before a down-swing became critical.

So it was that in 2011 I took early retirement from a local authority educational psychology service. I wanted to focus on freelance training and consultancy work, in the hope that this would give me a better work-life balance, and would free up more time for my family, and for myself. When you work in education, you never have a moment when you feel that your day's work is finished. There is always something more you could do, and I was still poor at putting my own needs above those I was trying to help.

I very much enjoyed the connections I made as a freelancer, with the trainees I supervised and the managers of the services they worked for. So it was for no particular reason that, when scrolling idly through social media a few years later, I replied to a Facebook post offering a house swap to Switzerland. It was one of those spur-of-the-moment impulses, just to see what it was about, and to dream a little. I had no actual desire to make such a radical change to my life.

However, the Swiss couple were delighted to hear from me. Before we could draw breath, they arranged to fly over to check out our house in Orkney, and their verdict was favourable. J had retired from his work and needed a fresh interest, and our children had all left home. There was nothing to hold us back.

3

FIRST STEPS OF DISCOVERY; SWITZERLAND, JANUARY 2014

So, we have come to live in Wil, a small town near Zurich in the German-speaking part of Switzerland, for six months. This feels like enough time to settle into the community, rather than just to take an extended holiday. I encounter a stumbling stone: although many do, not every Swiss person speaks English confidently. I take lessons in German, my father's birth tongue, but it is such a hard language! Word endings change arbitrarily, it seems to me, and noun genders bear no relationship to their owner and don't match up with the French language I learnt at school.

We settle into giving English classes, exploring our surroundings and making friends. Fresh impressions and new acquaintances follow each other with increasing rapidity.

I message Hans after the dinner party to say that my grandfather, Richard Landauer, a publisher, had moved from Munich to the Bavarian city of Landshut. My expectations that he would follow up on this information are low to non-existent; after all, many warm promises are made at the end of a convivial evening.

I am staggered by the email that arrives a few weeks later. Hans, a chance-met stranger, must have spent days searching the internet, sending emails and engaging with officialdom on my behalf. He has come back with so much information, I can hardly encompass it. As I read on, my heart swells and my brain swirls – dolphins ... grandfather's portrait in a collection ... club for stumbling stones ... world-famous cousin ... study done by researcher ... Where should I begin?

This is Hans' email to me:

> Looking for Dr Richard Landauer, you will find quite some information on the internet ... The publishing firm he owned was called *Delphin-Verlag* (Dolphin Publishing House).

It entrances me that my grandfather named his publishing company after the dolphin, a creature of the sea in which I swim throughout the year.

> Also, I found a collection of lithographic portraits of Munich publishers. Your grandfather's frontal portrait is found on page 4.

> Concerning a *'Stolperstein'* for your ancestors in Landshut: it appears there has been a public meeting of a club, in German a *'Verein'*, which concerns itself with the upkeep of the memories of Jewish citizens of Landshut. Its name is *Stolpersteine für Landshut – gegen das Vergessen e. V.* (Stumbling Stones for Landshut – Against Forgetting). The meeting was dedicated to the Landauer family. The speaker was Dr Barbara Schier, the author of a study on your grandfather's fate. I attach a translation ...

> There was another mention of Dr Richard Landauer ... that he also owned shares in other publishing companies, among them the famous *Jugend* (Youth) magazine, which gave name to the German variety of art deco, *Jugendstil*.

> There also seems to have been a brother [cousin, I discover later] of your grandfather's, Walter Landauer. He seems to

have emigrated to London earlier than Richard, to study design. He later went to the US (California), where he founded a company [Landor Associates] for design and advertising, which is still in business.

All in all, I think your chances of finding out more about your ancestors look pretty good. I suggest you might contact the *Stolpersteine Landshut – gegen das Vergessen e. V* and, with their help, Dr Barbara Schier ... She has probably already done most of the research that you intend to do. As mentioned in the announcement of the *Stolpersteine* club meeting, she seems to have been corresponding with Stephen Landor [my father's older brother]. Maybe she already passed copies of her findings to him? Whichever path you intend to follow in your quest, I would feel honoured to support you.

Hans' email is beyond anything I could imagine. I have become used to my German-ness being a cause of embarrassment, rather than interest. His offer to continue to support my search is touching and encouraging in equal measure. In just one page, he has already given me so many leads to pursue.

I begin by looking at his first attachment, the information about my grandfather's publishing company. I had not even known its name before.

The entry in the German Wikipedia says that Richard Landauer founded *Delphin-Verlag, München* in 1911 in Munich. I work out that Richard had created this business as a young man – before he was thirty, and before the start of the First World War in which he had served. I am impressed.

In the 1920s it published the series *Kleine Delphin-Kunstbücher* (Little Dolphin Art Books). The company's headquarters was moved to Landshut in 1933 and then deleted from the register in 1937. After this forced removal from the register, publishing was discontinued after 1945.

So, I muse, *Delphin-Verlag* had published a popular series whose name would be familiar to German readers – perhaps like our little Ladybird books – but then had been systematically forced out of business.

Verleger (Publisher)
Richard Landauer

The next attachment is the lithographic portrait. My grandfather was important enough to be included in a contemporary collection called *Münchner Köpfe* (Munich heads)! As was the custom of that time, Richard has a trimmed moustache beneath his nose. His lips are slightly parted, as if he is about to speak to the artist, and his gaze, behind round-lensed spectacles, is direct and intent. A receding hairline shows a large, square brow. Here is an intellectual, the portrait says, unflinching and aware. I wonder, though, whether the lithographer, Max Ludwig, intends to hint at Richard's Jewishness? Under the bridge of his glasses, the shading on the nose gives it a hint of a hook, more pronounced than it appears in contemporary photographs of him.

I can suddenly see a physical resemblance to my father's brother, Stefan. There would be no point in referring to my uncle for information, however, as I know he never speaks about his German Jewish background, whether through traumatic memories or shame, I'm not sure. In fact, I remember his teenage children asking my English mother, Margaret, to explain their heritage one Christmas when they were staying with us.

The Wikipedia article then cites the work of Dr Barbara Schier, a Munich sociologist and social psychologist: *Der Verlag Dr Richard Landauer. Eine Studie zur Ausschaltung eines jüdischen Verlegers im Dritten Reich* (The Publisher Dr Richard Landauer. A Study of the Elimination of a Jewish Publisher in the Third Reich).

Here is a mystery indeed. My grandfather was 'eliminated' in the Third Reich? I look up the German word *Ausschaltung* and come up with alternative translations: eviction, shutting down, eradication, subjugation. I understand then that she means his professional status as a publisher had been eliminated, not that he had been murdered like the six million victims of Nazi extermination. A mental shift is taking place in me: Richard Landauer was not just the distant, hardly known grandfather of my childhood; he had been a public figure who had accomplished much in his life, before his achievements were 'eliminated' by the Nazis.

I need time to reflect on all this new information, with mixed emotions of pride, interest and concern swirling around, before I can read on. My mind is buzzing with questions, so many questions – mostly about what my father had lost in the time before we, his children, existed …

Finally, I turn to the announcement of the meeting of the Landshut *Stolpersteine* association, which was to be addressed by Dr Barbara Schier, on 25 January 2013. The date of this meeting is just a year before the dinner party where we met Hans, and two days before the annual international Holocaust Day. The flier says 'The fate of the publisher's and merchant's family, who lived in Landshut from 1933 to 1938, shall be raised from oblivion'. It goes on to explain that the names of the five members of the Landauer family do not figure among those on the City of Landshut's list of twenty-four Jewish persons, for whom *Stolpersteine* were already planned; Dr Richard Landauer, his wife Edith, *née* Hirsch, and their children, Eva Maria, Stefan Klaus and [my father] Robert Felix, were not included. They wish 'to promote placement of five additional *Stolpersteine* at Theaterstrasse 55–57, next to those of Adolf and Cäcilie Hirsch [my great-grandparents]'.

It is hard to take this in. A year before I even know what a *Stolperstein* is, these stumbling stones, these jolts to memory, were already being proposed for my father, Robert, and his immediate family. And these were to be laid beside the ones previously planned for my great-grandparents. The good citizens of Landshut have rightly named their club 'Against Forgetting'.

There follows factual information about my grandparents, and about Richard's publishing firm *Delphin-Verlag*:

> Dr Richard Landauer had married Edith Hirsch, daughter of Adolf and Cäcilie Hirsch, owners of the Landshut department store known as *Kaufhaus Hermann Tietz Nachfolger*, on 27 March 1922 in Feldafing.

> In the years following the First World War, *Delphin-Verlag's* hallmark was a wide-ranging general programme with a specific focus on modern art and contemporary literature. Even in times of war and crisis, Richard Landauer published between twelve and twenty new titles. He seems, however, to have resigned early, even prior to the Machtergreifung [Nazi takeover of the *Deutsche Reich* government, 30 January 1933], due to the massive brutality of the Nazi activists.

My mind jumps to the scene in the film Cabaret where Natalie's little dog is found hanged. What had happened to my father's family?

> The Landauer family moved to Landshut on 10 October 1933 and lived in an apartment on the third floor above the department store *Hermann Tietz Nachfolger*.

Richard Landauer became one of the two directors of the department store.

From this account, I gather that *Delphin-Verlag* was a small, successful publishing company of modern art and literature but that its existence was threatened very early in the Nazi takeover. I guess that this was because Richard's area of specialism did not fit with Hitler's ideas of 'good' art, that which depicted classical Germanic heroes and rural Aryan folk bliss. Rather, *Delphin-Verlag* publications focused on what the Nazis called 'degenerate' art – that is, most modern expressionist or abstract artists such as Picasso, Dix and Kirchner. Richard had supported youth in art and the Art Deco movement, *Jugenstil*, in practical and public ways. It is widely understood that Hitler was a failed artist who felt rejected by the contemporary art world.

Richard's younger first cousin, Walter Landauer, born in Munich in 1913, also applied modern art to business when he established his famous design company, Landor Associates. Walter's father, Fritz Landauer, was a well-known architect who designed the liberal synagogue in Augsburg, making dramatic use of the new material, concrete. Bavaria's forward-looking art and culture surrounded the family. I learnt later that Richard regularly sent Walter art books and design magazines featuring *Werkbund* and *Bauhaus*, encouraging his passion for product design and branding. Walter, too, changed the spelling of his name from the Germanic Landauer to the English Landor. Walter Savage Landor had been a well-known poet and activist, friend of Charles Dickens and Robert Browning. His artistic merit and liberal republican politics may have encouraged the Landauers to adopt his name, rather than the more common English alternative, Lander. Walter left Germany to study in London in 1931, finally settling in San Francisco just as war broke out in Europe. He designed the brand identities for Coca-Cola, British Airways and Levi Strauss, among so many others; as he said, 'Products are made in the factory, but brands are created in the mind.' It warms me to think that my grandfather, Richard, encouraged the artistic development of his little cousin, leading to Walter's eventual world-wide fame.

In researching her monograph on Richard, Dr Schier contacted witnesses still living in Landshut, and also the former nursemaid of the Landauers, Anny Pitzl. She also corresponded with my uncle, Stefan Landauer, by then Dr Stephen Landor, in England.

Dr Schier also perused the extensive collection of correspondence that she found in the Bavarian State Archives. She found evidence of how difficult it had been for Dr Landauer to sell his publishing company to a non-Jewish German publisher. It took him from 1933 until early 1937 to sell *Delphin-Verlag* to *Böhlau Verlag* in Weimar for 15,000 *Reichsmark*, a heinously low price. This was achieved only just in time, because in April 1937, the German government's literature [i.e., censorship] department subjected all Jewish publishers to an occupational ban. *Delphin-Verlag* was deleted from the trade register on 1 April 1937. How severe this loss must have been, amidst the growing personal danger Richard would have felt for his young family.

To set this in context, February 1933 was dubbed 'the winter of literature', or rather perhaps the funeral of literature, as the NSDAP – the Nazi Party – attacked the liberal, permissive culture of the Weimar Republic. Well-known writers, artists and critics – Kurt Weil, Bertolt Brecht, Thomas Mann, Otto Dix, Georg Grosz, Alfred Kerr – were targeted for being Jews, communists, homosexuals or 'degenerates'. Their work was banned, their professional positions removed, and their books burned in huge bonfires whose reeking smoke filled the streets. Many of them fled from Germany. Dr Schier had written:

> Richard Landauer had moved to Landshut as early as October 1933, probably to seek Adolf Hirsch's protection for his family. Adolf was a highly respected and popular

Landshut citizen. He was an honorary member of the traditional Landshut sports club [the social equivalent of the Rotary Club in the UK, perhaps] from 1919, and benefactor of numerous social institutions in Landshut. On 19 September 1938 the Landauer family de-registered from the police file of Landshut inhabitants with the destination address of 17 Parsifal Road, London. How the Landauer family fared in the following years, you may find out by attending the 25 January meeting.

There is an inordinate amount of information to take in from this flier, so kindly translated by our new friend, Hans, containing many avenues to learning more about my patrimony. I peruse it again and again, along with Hans' other attachments. Here is far more loss and trauma than my mind can encompass – or cope with. I had supposed that an interest in my father's family was personal, and relevant to me alone; now I feel amazed that their fate was a hook for Landshut inhabitants to attend a public meeting.

My first step must be to email the organisers of the *Stolpersteine für Landshut* organisation, and Dr Barbara Schier. Perhaps they might be willing to help me connect with my family's German past.

4

MUNICH, FEBRUARY 2014

The dinner party is one of several invitations from the neighbours and families of our house-swappers, who take it upon themselves to introduce us to the delights of living in the heart of the European continent. We explore our new environment with enthusiasm, firstly in their company and then more independently as we grow in confidence. Switzerland is far closer to Germany than is our home in Orkney, so we make the journey to my father's country of birth several times during our six-month house exchange. We have been lent our house-swappers' car, with its local number plates, and are usually able to drive straight through the unmanned border posts. On one occasion though, a customs officer waves us in to the side of the road on our return to Switzerland. He peers through the car windows, front and rear.

'*Bitte–*'

J interrupts him.

'We're from Scotland. I'm sorry, we only speak English.'

'*Ach so.* Please open your trunk for my inspection.'

At the sight of our meagre haul in the car boot – a small pack of *Bratwurst* and another of Westphalian ham – the officer breaks into a broad grin.

'This is all you have bought? Swiss people fill their trunks at the cheap German supermarkets and try to bring it all home; but there is a legal limit, you know.'

He waves us on our way, chuckling to himself at our Scottish parsimony.

One of our excursions is to Munich, with other family members who are visiting, and we all enjoy exploring its parks and streets. We see *Romeo and Juliet* at the beautiful neo-classical Munich Opera House. I buy stout German walking boots at a specialist shop. Our spacious rented flat has five large bedrooms, with high ceilings and wooden floors. It is inhabited by some young women who clear out to visit their boyfriends whenever they need the extra income to be made from subletting.

The Landauers' apartment until 1933, Elisabethstrasse, Munich

My personal pilgrimage to *Elisabethstrasse*, to see and photograph the apartment building where my father lived for his first six years, makes a big impression on me. The first floor of the cream-plastered building extends slightly over the street, with shapely supporting structures and tall windows. There is no point ringing the doorbell as I can't explain the reason for my visit in German; I content myself with imagining from street level the lofty rooms and velvet drapes that had once hidden my infant father. It is pleasant to walk along the wide, tree-lined street, with a small park, cafes and shops at one end. Outside a nearby bar, a horse-drawn cart delivers barrels of beer with loud thuds, the aroma of strong coffee and *Bienenstich* honey cakes wafting from the open door. I imagine Anny, the Landauers' nursemaid, taking my father's hand as she walked him and his older siblings along this same street.

Following up on Hans' email, I contact Dr Barbara Schier, and she invites us to an exquisite afternoon tea in her apartment. There are dainty sandwiches and little German speciality cakes, white wine served in crystal glasses and white tea in bone china cups. My lack of German and hers of English is a barrier to direct communication, but some of my other family members have better language skills and can translate between us. Dr Schier explains that she planned to focus her doctoral research on my grandfather Richard's *Delphin-Verlag* but was unable to find the publishing company archives. She asks us if we, his family, have these records? Without them, she could not write her full thesis on his story and only produced a monograph with what material she could find. She gives us a copy. Unfortunately, we know nothing about the whereabouts of the *Delphin-Verlag* archive. Indeed, a few short months ago we knew nothing about *Delphin-Verlag*.

I have visited Munich twice before. My very first glimpse of my father's birthplace was confined to the railway station, where we arrived off the London sleeper train when I was six. We were on our way to Feldafing to visit my grandfather – the only time I met him. The station was a mighty cavern, filled with hissing steam and groaning brakes from the locomotives, and the rattle of porters' trolleys. Black-hatted men in heavy wool coats thronged the concourse. The pervasive smell of their continental tobacco was so exotic compared to the St Bruno Flake my English grandad favoured.

Then, when I was eleven, on a family Dormobile holiday to Interlaken, we stopped in Munich to visit Anny Pitzl, our father's childhood nursemaid. My first taste of her baked cheesecake, not too sour and not too sweet, brought back memories of visiting Aunt Liesel and the other elderly German relatives in London a few years previously. My mother tried to help Anny clear up our plates and take them to the kitchen.

'*Pass auf!*' Anny cried as she rescued the tottering pile.

As we left, Margaret said to Robert in hurt tones,

'You said Anny had no English, but she said 'Buzz off' to me, as clear as anything, when I went into her kitchen.'

"*Pass auf!*' my father corrected her, smiling. "*Pass auf* means 'Look out!' 'Be careful!'"

Language can indeed be a stone to stumble over. (On another occasion, my mother served up the mushrooms she had foraged, having translated the German fungi book's *etwas giftig* – slightly poisonous – as 'very tasty', an error my father also laughed off affectionately.)

Munich was my father's cradle. There, he was the adored youngest son, heir to art and culture, taken through the wide, leafy boulevards by their nursemaid. Robert's middle name was Felix, which is Latin for happy, and he lived up to it throughout his life until his final years. His childhood nickname was *Floh* (flea); it sounds as if he was an irrepressible and cheerful little boy, who knew how to get the attention every child needs.

Throughout the 1920s, it must have seemed to Richard that he had it all. He was sharing his passion for modern art and literature with a public who was hungry for his books. In his forties by then, he was well established and respected, a successful proprietor and loyal German citizen, and husband and father to a delightful family. Despite the growing anti-Semitism of the time, no one could have foreseen how tragically this was about to change for him.

As a person ages, there is often a growing need to prepare for the end of life and make peace with the past. In India an elderly person may dye their hair with henna, renouncing home, family and possessions, to focus on their spiritual growth. Many turn to the creative arts in retirement, to explore the significance of a life almost done. Recently there has been an explosion in DNA testing, alongside the 'Who Do You Think You Are?' type of popular TV heredity programme.

The Orkney archipelago, where I live, lies just a few miles off John O'Groats, the northernmost tip of Britain's mainland. Prevailing south-westerly winds dominate these islands with an almost constant presence. Trees are sculpted by the airflow over surrounding buildings, as if a giant's knife has sheared them. Every summer, Orkney is host to countless visitors looking up their ancestry, visiting archives and church graveyards, and seeking relatives through Facebook posts – though their family's diaspora usually resulted from economic need rather than war. Orcadians are seafarers and have always journeyed outward, beyond the horizons of the surrounding waters. For a place with a present-day population of only twenty-two thousand, Orkney is surprisingly well-known: for its World Heritage status as the Neolithic heartland and for the Italian Chapel of the Second World War; for the seaweed-eating North Ronaldsay sheep and for the scuttled German fleet lying under the waters of Scapa Flow; for the writing of George Mackay Brown and for the music of Orkney-based composer, Sir Peter Maxwell Davies; for the rare *primula scottica* and the Orkney vole; for green pasture and sandy bays.

And now it is my turn. I too am asking myself, what snakes, what ladders made me whom I have become? Others – Australians and New

Zealanders, Americans and Canadians – flock to Orkney in search of their roots. Here, where I've made my home for the past four decades, I'm swimming against the tide. I'm reaching outwards from Orkney, whilst also looking inwards to my psyche.

I have spent my working life trying to help people learn. I have, at different times, focused on teaching English as a foreign language, supporting learning in primary and secondary schools, behaviour support, preschool special needs, and educational psychology. It occurs to me now that I might use the knowledge I have gained to help me reflect on my own developmental trajectory.

For example, I read in my studies of education that learning is most successful when there is a sensitive balance between support and challenge. If a child is supported the whole time, they do not need to grow, to learn and to develop new skills of independence; everything is being done for them. On the other hand, if they are always being corrected or challenged, they will need to protect themselves from what can feel like a sustained attack, and they will resist. Imagine how a hedgehog will refuse to move forward when poked or threatened, instead curling into a ball and presenting defensive spines. A good teacher will judge when to give help and when to exhort, when to step back and when to push, taking into account the individual's personality, context and past experience. This is the way to build confidence and resilience, the capacity to get back up after a stumble.

Did the rocks in my path diminish or strengthen me? How was I helped to get back up again? My parents, and their parents, had barriers in their lives that differed from mine. They survived war, genocide, displacement and death of their loved ones. Some stumbling stones must have curtailed potential in each of us, while others built in us the ability to survive, and even to thrive.

My parents came from contrasting backgrounds. My father, Robert, was born in 1927, the third child of Richard Landauer, a successful Munich art book publisher, and his wife Edith, *née* Hirsch. At some point between our ancestor in the nineteenth century, Moses Samuel Landauer, who practised the Jewish faith, and Richard Landauer in the twentieth century, the family left the Jewish religious community and adopted Germany's mainstream Christian faith. The best examples of classical and modern art, culture, and design surrounded Robert in his early childhood. My father was always humming or whistling melodies from Vivaldi or Bach, and he loved to take me to classical concerts. By the time I was nine or ten, he was the one with whom I could share my feelings and ideas. He was a cheerful, optimistic and idealistic man, wanting to serve humanity.

My mother, Margaret, was the more down-to-earth of the pair. She was an only child, born in 1928, after seven years of marriage and several miscarriages, to Fred and Mabel Kirkland, of Ashbourne, Derbyshire, by then in their mid-thirties. Fred worked behind the cheese counter of a village cooperative shop all his life, and both he and Mabel had had to leave school at fourteen to go out to work. Mabel had ambitions for Margaret. She organised piano lessons for her, which would otherwise have been unaffordable, by allowing the music teacher to use their front room for giving lessons. She wanted her daughter to experience the wider world, encouraging her friendship with a Dutch penfriend, but lacked the means to do more. Then when the time came, she encouraged Margaret to fulfil her own unattained ambition – to stay on at school and to attend teacher training college. Her daughter was the first in their wider family to achieve higher education.

Both my grandfathers, Richard and Fred, had served in the First World War, though on opposing sides. Richard was a lieutenant, awarded the German Empire's *Eisernes Kreuz*, the Iron Cross. It was unusual for a Jewish person to achieve officer status in that era. Like the protagonist of Morpurgo's *War Horse*, my other grandfather, Fred, was a groom; he served in The Derbyshire Yeomanry, a cavalry and infantry division.

My father, Robert, had died at the shockingly young age of fifty-nine but his failing mind had meant he had been absent from us for seven years before that. Margaret lived on for another fourteen years, before dying from cancer at seventy-one. They both died so young, burnt out perhaps from their eventful lives. I have already had over a decade more life than my father and have overtaken my mother's lifespan. This awareness spurs my reflections about my place in this succession; I am the product of a love match between two people of vastly different cultures and backgrounds, who nevertheless must have found a kindred spirit in each other.

5

MOTHER DAUGHTER RELATIONSHIP; DERBYSHIRE, 1961

I remember sitting on the front doorstep, enjoying a burst of sunshine at the tender start of a Derbyshire summer. I must have been about eight. Hoverflies hummed over yellow berberis flowers, the scent of sweet peas filled the air and wood pigeons' throaty burbling punctuated the shimmering morning. I was wearing a short-sleeved cotton dress. In the crooks of my elbows and the inside of each shin meandered long, white scars, puckered and raised above my flesh. I was at the age to begin comparing my body to others'. And no one else I knew was marked in such a way – not my friends at school, not my brother, parents or grandparents ...

I asked my mother, 'What are these lines?'

'Those are where you had a blood transfusion when you were a baby.'

When I was born in the early 1950s, I had what they then knew as 'rhesus complications', she explained. She told me that rhesus is a condition where the mother's blood produces antibodies that fight the blood of the unborn infant.

'Babies always carry the father's blood type. And if the parents' blood types are incompatible, like Dad's and mine were, the mother's blood produces antibodies in reaction to the birth of the first child, so the second child gets sick. We didn't know any of that until you were born, when you were so ill.'

At that time, the medics in Macclesfield Hospital were experimenting with different treatment methods for rhesus babies like me; they took me in for blood 'boosters' each time I became seriously ill. I learnt that my older brother, Mark, was a bonny, healthy babe, whereas I spent my first year of life in and out of hospital, as my blood counts repeatedly plunged to life-threatening levels. They gave me endless shots of healthy blood, hoping my system would respond by overcoming the lethal antibodies. They also gave me huge doses of iron; when my baby teeth appeared, they were black. When I was one year old, my mother explained, they gave up on this experiment and took me in for a total blood transfusion. And I still have those scars on my ankles and elbows, over six decades later.

This account of my illness and recovery is not in accord with modern scientific knowledge; both terminology and treatment around rhesus have changed. But it was what framed our interpretation of our very first relationship as mother and daughter, and, indeed, of the start of my parents' marriage.

She had fallen pregnant with my brother, Mark, a few months after their wedding, and I was born two years after him. German Jewish refugee Robert and English Protestant Margaret had fallen in love across cultures, in the aftermath of a cataclysmic world war. Did this scrawny, sick rhesus baby feel like the physical manifestation of their mixed marriage, of the chasm between their innate conditions? The blood of two races was mingling after long centuries of hatred, and my English mother's Protestant blood was rejecting my father's Jewish blood that was present in his baby. And for my young mother, whose first child had been born only a few days before her twenty-first birthday – how must it have felt to survive a world war, begin your 'happy ever after', and then be told that your own blood was killing your baby? She was an only child herself; was this a judgement on her hubris of wanting a second child? On the other hand, the war was over, and it was time to look forward. Nothing could be as bad as the last two decades, with all their pain and loss. The National Health Service was now five years old and would provide every citizen with all the medical care they needed, paid for through taxation, regardless of wealth or age. The information leaflet had said:

> It will provide you with all medical, dental and nursing care. Everyone – rich or poor, man, woman or child – can use it or any part of it. There are no charges, except for a few special items. There are no insurance qualifications. But it is not a 'charity'. You are all paying for it, mainly as taxpayers, and it will relieve your money worries in time of illness.

Even though they had a sick baby, at least they were free from worry about paying for her care.

Now, seventy years later, I can't know their thoughts and feelings. I can only imagine, and try to deduce, falling back on my professional knowledge of psychology to help me dig a little deeper.

When the rhesus positive and negative human blood types were discovered in the 1930s, they were wrongly thought to be the same as rhesus monkey antigens, hence the name. It was common to use rhesus monkeys in medical research in that era.

I remain haunted by the textbook photographs of Harry Harlow's huge-eyed little rhesus monkey, in his psychological experiments of the 1960s. The baby had been taken from its mother at birth and reared in a cage with two wire-mesh, surrogate-mother frames; one frame was padded in a soft fabric while the other dispensed milk through a bottle and tube. The infant monkey spent most of its time clinging onto the soft frame, only visiting the bare wire frame when it needed to feed. Baby monkeys who were only given the milk-dispensing, wire-mesh surrogate failed to thrive, and died.

From this, psychologists began to understand that infants also need love and comfort for survival, not just to have their basic nutritional needs met. In later experiments, the baby monkey would explore a new surrounding with confidence if the soft frame was present; if they took this surrogate mother away, the baby would show signs of extreme distress, rocking and screaming, or withdrawing into itself.

Did I rock and scream, or withdraw into silence, during those countless hospital stays? My parents would not have known, as in those days parents were not allowed to stay with their children in hospital. Visiting was discouraged, lest it unsettle the infant patient. In any case, their home village, Rainow, was some three miles from Macclesfield, and they had a two-year-old to look after, along with my father's demanding job as a probation officer.

They took me back to that hospital on a visit when I was six.

'See how well she is? We just came to show you, and to thank you for saving her life.'

Nurses and doctors knelt down to engage with me, but my heart was pounding and my ears let no words into my brain. I had been too young to remember anything, my parents believed; yet I was feeling completely frozen, terrified and nauseated by the hospital smell. Bodies recall trauma when brains cannot. I wonder how much my current anxiety reaction to stress stems from this early and repeated experience of painful procedures and separation? Since my infancy, psychologists such as John Bowlby have taught us more about the impact of early attachment on development and wellbeing. In order to survive, the helpless human infant must seek proximity to a care-giving adult and form a close relationship with them. The primary caregiver – in those days always termed the mother – is then invested in keeping the baby safe and nourished, because of this close bond. Babies smile and babble engagingly when their needs are being met, and show distress when separated.

Research shows that in most languages throughout the world, babies' first name for their mother is mama, mummy, and so on, and for their father it is baba, dada, papa. 'Mmmaa' is the natural sound of complaint and distress, and expresses to the mother the need for nurture and for feeding. B/d/p are the sounds produced in cheerful babble when playing, which engages the father in a rewarding interaction. This encourages him to stay around to protect the mother and the child, who carries his genes, with his superior physical strength.

Mary Ainsworth, another developmental psychologist and a colleague of Bowlby, built on these studies. She showed that only infants who are secure in their first attachment relationship will explore new surroundings, thus furthering their opportunities for learning and development. This stress on the importance of the maternal role suited the political priorities of the post-war era. Women had taken on traditional men's work during the war, driving lorries and tilling the land, but now in peacetime the men needed their jobs back. Their wives were being encouraged back to the home, to look after the children and keep house. I wonder whether my mother felt torn between caring for her young family, or supplementing their income and maintaining her own development as a professional? In my first year of life, I had suffered repeated breaks in my prime attachment relationship with my parents. If any child now needed stability, it was surely this one.

Before my mother died in 2000, I mostly saw her faults. I feared I was repeating them – snapping at family members when under stress, using food and alcohol as a crutch – and I hated feeling I was 'turning out like her'. Both she and I ended up overweight in middle age and were often rather too 'relaxed' by the end of an evening.

I remember one occasion in the mid-1990s when, unusually in Orkney's maritime Gulf Stream climate, it had snowed during one of my mother's visits. We were nursing mugs of hot coffee while we watched the children rolling a gigantic ball, the body for a snowman. The appetising aroma drifted towards our nostrils as wisps of steam rose in the crisp, still air. My mother suddenly said,

'You know, I was thinking about that time I stuffed snow into your little wellies when we were on a walk ... What a dreadful thing to do! I feel so guilty.'

I laughed. It was a very long time ago.

'Yes, I remember it well! I was complaining that my feet were so cold they hurt, and you must have got fed up with my whining ... '

It was true, I did feel the cold, having spent most of my childhood in Africa, and clothing wasn't as weatherproof in the early 1960s in England.

'And,' I continued, 'there was that time you wouldn't cut up my beans on toast when I had a friend to tea, and you mocked me for asking. I'd fallen out of a tree and sprained my wrist, you know!'

She winced. We smiled together wryly over these instances of her parenting failures but didn't take the conversation any deeper. Neither she nor I had developed the habit of honest reflection or discussion. It is only now, half a lifetime later, that I am trying to understand a little more.

When my mother was growing up, it wasn't good practice to praise children, and modesty, rather than self-confidence, was what parents strove to instil. This generational difference showed up clearly on another occasion. My mother was visiting us when my young children were on a 'learn to ski' week at the dry ski-slope outside Edinburgh. I couldn't help remarking how lovely my little daughter looked, as she carefully snow-ploughed down the baby slope.

Margaret said,

'And doesn't she know it! You keep telling her ... '

Something snapped, and I retorted,

'It's more of a shame that I wasn't made to feel confident about how I looked when I was growing up.'

This was the only time I had openly criticised her over my upbringing; she flinched, and we backed off this sensitive topic. I must have had a deep well of unconscious resentment at feeling I'd been abandoned, in infancy and many times again through childhood, which I had never discussed with her. How could I, when I had never even expressed these feelings to myself?

As a teenager, I hated the way I looked. When friends gathered at our house to watch the innovative American TV show, *Rowan and Martin's Laugh-in*, I felt embarrassed whenever Ruth Buzzi appeared in a sketch; I knew they were laughing at her large, jutting chin. (Many years later, I confessed this fear to a friend who looked startled; he had always assumed they were laughing at her big nose, which was the same as his, he thought ...). Like Buzzi, I have a Habsburg jaw, which our childhood dentist tried to cure with uncomfortable dental plates, a painful and perpetual reminder of my disfigurement. The torturing plate spent quite a lot of time hidden in my trouser pocket, or falling out and getting broken, but it was always replaced with a new one.

Confusingly, while I think I am the only one of my siblings who grew up with chronic issues about my face and body from my mother's strictures – 'Don't stick your chin out! Don't round your shoulders!' – I am also the only one with a large oil portrait, commissioned by my mother when I was about eight. Did she think I looked nice, beautiful even, but could never say so? Her usual way was to puncture pretension with humour.

'Look at this photo, Mum, look – I *have* got a waist!' I said in wonder when I was fifteen, poring over a holiday snap.

'Yes dear, you have a lovely figure – it's just that you walk so funny ...'

46

In childhood I noticed how kind she was to my friends, whilst holding me to far higher standards; she used a different, softer voice when speaking to them. I think I must have been a timid, needy child, irritating in my over-sensitivity. With the distance of age, it occurs to me now that she might have wanted me to be brave and cheerful, to overcome whatever life could fling at me. Perhaps she wanted to protect me by encouraging me to toughen up. After all, she herself had made courageous life choices, in the face of cataclysmic change and hardship.

We mothers have no idea of our power. Have I in turn damaged my own children whom I love more than I can say? (Note to self: I must try to express this love more openly, more often, more warmly ...)

6

DELVING DEEPER; SWITZERLAND, FEBRUARY 2014

The next email from Hans bears a lengthy attachment; with care and persistence, he has rendered a clear translation of the somewhat dense academic text of Dr Schier's monograph. There is so much information about my grandfather to take in.

I learn that in the time leading up to World War One and afterwards, *Delphin-Verlag* ranked among Munich's smaller publishing houses. However, its wide range of publications specialising in modern art and contemporary literature placed it in the 'popular books' (*Publikumsverlag*) sector. Munich was a centre for progressive social and psychological thinking at the turn of the twentieth century. Indeed, publisher Hans Weber stated in 1917 that Dr Landauer enjoyed

> ... great professional renown as the founder and sole proprietor of a publishing house of high artistic standards, not only among his fellow publishers, [but] also among connoisseurs of art and literature ...

So, my grandfather's peers had appreciated his life work, as had the public, it seems.

Dr Schier also states that one of Dr Landauer's explicit intentions was to make modern art known to the public. This, she writes, can be seen from the list of titles he published (*Verlagsbibliographie*). They covered an astonishingly wide range of topics, even during the First World War and the ensuing economic crisis:

Delphin-Verlag was a potent, trend-setting, modern publishing house, whose management knew how to tend to low-budget customers, as well as the well-to-do for whom it offered leather-bound luxury editions.

It seemed that Richard was not just concerned with making a living, but had a higher goal, a passion: to share his love of art with his people.

When Richard died in 1960, *Aufbau*, the well-known New York newspaper for German emigrants, printed this obituary, describing him as

> ... one of us, whose view on life was different from that of his fathers – one of the rare seekers, an explainer, an unerring, upright idealist. His aim was to trace the artistic and literary currents of his time, which heralded a profound upheaval, to explain them and to make the public familiar with them.

This was the man who had earned my seven-year-old self's undying gratitude for sending me a working miniature washing machine for my dolls' clothes. My childhood grandfather, who gave a little girl such wonderful presents in the parsimonious 1950s, was a man of international renown! I can feel pride welling within me, and I can also see where my father's desire to serve humanity sprang from.

Dr Schier concludes her monograph with this summary:

> The books published by Dr Landauer characterise him, they are testimony of his work, his ambitions, his personality ... In the obituaries, his return to Germany is generally interpreted as an indication of his inseverable and close relationship to his *Heimat* (homeland).

My uncle Stephen wrote to Dr Schier that his father had returned to Germany because 'German was the language he loved, and he was a typically intellectual German and never felt at home in England.' Despite the enormous harm and hurt caused to Richard and his family over the past twenty years, in his old age he could only feel comfortable in the land of his birth, where he had spent the best years of his life. His roots were in Bavaria. Perhaps despite, perhaps because of my peripatetic childhood, it occurs to me that my desire never to leave my adopted home, Orkney, is because I have at last laid down roots.

In another piece of serendipity, my cousin Karen mentions that she has inherited a pack of family letters from her father, Stephen. He had found them when clearing out his sister Eva's flat after her death. The letters date from the late 1940s, she thinks, and the pack includes lots of random scraps.

We arrange for her to post the pack to me, and in due course it arrives. As she warned, there are many oddments that have lost any meaning by now. A stash of aged and battered rosettes, never thrown away, bring a lump to my throat, however. Eva loved horses and fulfilled her longing for riding by volunteering at weekends with the Civil Service's stables. I knew she had groomed and mucked out the horses, with the occasional ride in Hyde Park as a reward, but here was evidence that she had also competed – and successfully.

Around half the personal letters are to Eva; two are from Robert, several are from American friends about her trip to the States, and one is from the young woman who would marry Robert and become my mother. To my surprise, there are also half a dozen letters written by my father but not to Eva – to his brother Stephen and his new wife Phyllis. Just the sight of his neat, forward-sloping hand, so familiar from the weekly letters that were my crutch at boarding school, clenches at my heart. It is commonly supposed that small handwriting denotes an introverted personality, but this was not true in my father's case. He was sunny and outgoing in his prime. I could only suppose that his careful handwriting was the product of his German upbringing. He also ate slowly, chewing every mouthful thoroughly before swallowing, another sign of a long-gone child-rearing practice. Born in 1849, Horace Fletcher 'The Great Masticator' recommended that, before it was swallowed, food should be masticated until it became liquid, and his advice was followed all over the world.

Robert typed most of his letters, adding a few handwritten lines to sign off. He mostly wrote them in 1947 and 1948, with one last letter to notify them of the birth of my brother Mark in 1950. Had Eva selected these few and thrown away others? Would that there were more hoarders in the world, I muse.

I read through them quickly, then read them all again, savouring each one. Through my work as an educational psychologist, I know about the important link between writing by hand and learning: the repetitive hand movements give a physical, or kinaesthetic, reinforcement to visual memory. I am also rediscovering for myself the benefits of writing by hand for freeing the creative flow, since treating myself to a paper tablet. But I had forgotten how visceral is the sight of a loved one's handwriting.

During these years just after the end of the Second World War, both Karen's parents and mine were busy establishing their careers and relationships with their eventual life partners. I think myself back to that time in my own life; I spent the year after finishing university living in London, attending teacher training college and strengthening the relationship with the man who would become my husband.

My first task on receiving the pack of letters is to have them professionally photocopied, and then I spend some time transcribing each one. These letters are going to be shared with other family members and treasured. Most precious is the gift of getting to know my father as a young man, before his demobilisation and his marriage – and before we children were part of his world.

Robert died aged only fifty-nine, almost thirty years before I saw these letters, and he had been fading from us for seven years before that. In those days, his sudden decline was called 'premature senility', an ugly label for such a relatively young man. The word 'senile' carried connotations of an ancient, wandering idiot whose mind has long gone. Where was my dad, who could thrash younger men at badminton and hold in mind his own and everyone else's game at Scrabble? He had indeed disappeared.

Through our aunt's safekeeping and my cousin's gift, I have just gained access to some extra years of Robert's too-short life. It was serendipity that gave me the initial contact with Hans, leading me to a network of connections established through his active efforts on my behalf. Now I have more source information that was written by my own father, in English, and this energises me. I can move from being a passive recipient of the kind efforts of others, to becoming active in pursuing my own goal of discovering my family roots. I spend the next decade in close study, following up addresses and researching contemporary events. In this way, I can build a clearer picture of who my father and his family were, and of where I have come from.

I sort through the envelope of papers my cousin has sent me and extract the letters from my father. Most of them were written during his period of national service, when he worked with German and Austrian prisoners of war held at Scraptoft Camp, Leicester, making use of his birth language. His role was to interview the prisoners of war, contributing to an assessment of the threat level they posed and to their type and level of need; this information was required so they could be repatriated as soon as possible. It seems like a very complex and responsible job for such a young man, but it was good preparation for his eventual career as a probation officer. At least he did not have to see active service, as had his own father Richard, and Fred Kirkland, the father of his fiancée Margaret, in the previous world war.

How much can be learnt from a good letter! The person presented in the letters from my father feels half familiar – I can hear his voice and see his ready smile – but also half new. Over months of reading, re-reading and transcribing, I pore over many aspects of the bright young man he was. It feels strange to consider that he was twenty then, and I am now the age his grandmother Cilly would then have been had she survived the Holocaust.

Most of these letters were written to his brother Stefan, by now always known as Stephen, and his new wife. Stephen and Phyllis, both chemists, had met each other during their national service; they were working in the ICI laboratories in Welwyn Garden City alongside Dr John Crawford, the man who developed the shatterproof Perspex used in aircraft windows.

While carrying out his national service, Robert was also looking to his future and working towards qualifications that would enable him to enter higher education. In Robert's letter of October 1947, addressed from the Hipswell Lodge training centre, we see him trying to keep up, through every means possible, with the education a twenty-year-old would have had in normal times. He obviously enjoyed writing and made his letters both entertaining and informative:

> To make things easier, let me, like the crab, go backwards and start with the most recent events first. One of those is a very mediocre dinner just consumed, cooked by Pioneer cooks, and as I'm now used to POW [prisoner of war] cooking, I've become fussy.

The Pioneer Corps, formed in 1939 and nicknamed 'The King's Most Loyal Enemy Aliens', accepted German and Austrian refugees and was established for light engineering duties. It was clear that their training did not include cuisine.

Robert wrote:

> This morning the course started and, quite reasonably, our instructors, who consist of one elderly civilian, the 'Director of Studies' and two Education Corps Sergeants, set the ball rolling by trying to find out what we did not know. And we soon supplied them with the proof (if proof were needed) of our ignorance, confirming their worst fears. Specifically, the mathematics test was the downfall of most of the 28 of us, and according to that we have been divided into two groups, or syndicates as they call them here. The queer thing is that most people on this course are of a fairly high intellectual standard, but for some unknown reason have not matriculated. Anyway, as far as I can see this course means business, and I'll have to work damn hard to try and keep up with my correspondence courses, which I took with me.

Robert's greatest attribute was to engage with anyone and everyone, showing a genuine interest in them, and his listening skills drew people to him:

> I was up at 3 a.m. to send off some Ps/W [prisoners of war], stayed at the station to catch a train to Leeds, then to Doncaster, then to York, then to Darlington, then to Richmond, then cycled to camp, had tea and then came here – well, I expect even you feel tired by now, and you didn't have to do it. However, there's always something to be

gained from everything, and I met quite an interesting lad on the train. He had just got his Higher School Certificate, was going to take chemistry next year, and, if allowed to defer, take his B.Sc. ...

Instead of complaining about such an arduous work schedule, he always found the best in every situation:

Repatriation is going to be speeded up in the individual camps, but many are going to close, so the overall rate won't increase. We shall get 2000 Ps/W passing through our camp every week, which does mean rather more work, though the machinery for repatriation has been simplified. Worst of all, it means getting up at about four o'clock in the morning twice every week – I don't fancy that at all. But it might be worse.

' ...there's always something to be gained from everything ... ' 'I met quite an interesting lad ... ' ' ... it might be worse.' My father's middle name, Felix, was appropriate; he had a cheerful, caring personality which boosted the morale of those around him.

As I read and re-read, this young Robert, his confidence and passions, his humour and care for others is, at last, overlaying the memory of what he became at the end: a shambling, speechless man who kept to the shadows as he slowly diminished towards death. It is common to regret not paying more attention to our parents' lived experience, when we are so busy making our own way. By the time we have leisure to reflect on our inheritance, it is often too late. My long-held feelings of rootlessness are being assuaged by the unexpected gift of this pack of letters, which are allowing me to get to know this young man, my father.

7

YOUNG LOVE; LETTERS, 1947 – 1949

In the letter of October 1947, Robert also referred to the recent marriage of Stephen and Phyllis, which took place in the Friends Meeting House at Welwyn Garden City. Quakers have always welcomed refugees, and Robert felt drawn to their pacifist and egalitarian philosophy. No clergy officiate at Sunday worship in a Quaker meeting. The meeting room is simple and unadorned, and the Friends sit together to reflect in silence, unless someone is moved to stand up and express their thoughts aloud. It could not differ more completely from the ancient liturgy and opulence of a Catholic service that the family would have been used to in Germany. Stephen and Phyllis had no religious belief themselves, and so chose not to have a conventional church wedding, opting instead for their younger brother's community of faith.

Robert delicately alluded to their father's response to the occasion in his letter to Stephen:

> What, by the way, did Father think of the wedding? Or perhaps this is a question that Eva might answer more easily, as Father may not have been quite frank with you. I have the impression that he did like it very much, but might have felt a little 'out of it'. He was in a very bad mood after you had left, and was near crying in the bus. I'm afraid I never said a word of what he wanted me to say, nor was what I did say during the meeting what he perhaps expected. I wonder whether he'll perhaps understand our way of thinking and our beliefs a little better now that you are living at home.

Stephen and Phyllis were to start their married life in one part of the two-storey apartment in Goldhurst Terrace. What might Richard have felt, sitting on that bus? I am letting my imagination roam … I guess he may have been remembering his own wedding, which took place on 27 March 1922 in Feldafing. Eighteen years older than Edith, his bride, he was deeply in love and worshipped her in every way possible; their first child, Eva, was born on 26 December 1922, precisely nine months after their wedding day. Perhaps he found this focus on 'friends' rather chilly and devoid of passion as he understood it. He may have been looking for the attention to the senses and artistic sensibility that would have marked his own wedding. A Friends Meeting House probably seemed to him a bare and draughty place, compared to a beautiful Bavarian Catholic church, with no music or art to raise one's spirits and no priest orating in a time-honoured ritual. Attending their son's wedding must have made him miss his own wife so badly. She had died less than five years previously – she should have been there, beside him.

As well as being drawn to the simple austerity of Quakerism, the father I remember loved popular chamber music, in particular Vivaldi. He explained to me once that ordinary people making music in their own homes would have enjoyed such music. To him, it seemed both intimate and egalitarian – very like a Friends Meeting in concept.

On clearing our mother's bedroom after her death, we found in her wedding ring case a tiny, embossed paper horseshoe and a folded paper, on which Robert had written out the vow he had made at their wedding in Leicester Meeting House on 6 August 1949:

> Friends, I take this my friend Margaret Kirkland to be my wife, promising, through Divine assistance, and as long as we both on earth shall live, to be unto her a loving and faithful husband. Love is the greatest factor in Life, it is that which gives Life its beauty; it is the spring of human

nobleness, the essence of all good, it is the condition of happiness. Therefore, have faith in Life at its best, and bring to it your courage, your hopes and your sense of humour.

She had kept it safe all through her years of marriage and widowhood. His handwriting as always is small, neat, and forward sloping, as if he is rushing with determination and purpose to meet all that life can offer.

As the oldest, Mark was an executor of our mother's will. Among her effects, he found two handmade cards wrapped in tissue paper, from the period when our parents were courting. He sends them to me now, to add to the pack of letters Karen gave me. The first one was a card for her twentieth birthday, on 27 September 1948. Robert had made it from a large sheet of stiff art paper, folded in four, and had written in careful script on the front cover:

To my love on this 27th day of September 1948, Happy Birthday, Margaret, and the blessing of all the Richness of Life! Be strong, courageous, patient – be gay and joyful, answering the good in everyone; be happy! I ask little else but that I may contribute to that. With all love, your Robin.

I was interested to see that he still capitalised some nouns, perhaps to give them emphasis or perhaps as a remnant of his birth language, German. Under this, he had copied out Shakespeare's Sonnet 128, where the poet wishes he were the musical instrument fingered and blown by his loved one, lines full of suggestive imagery:

Since saucy jacks so happy are in this,

Give them thy fingers, me thy lips to kiss.

The next page has a black-and-white photo of the Venus de Milo glued to it, which Robert had labelled as the Greek god Aphrodite.

On the following page, he translated some lines written by Friedrich Rickert, which are the words of Franz Schubert's Lied no. 3 of 1823:

> Thou art repose, mild peace,
> Thou art yearning,
> And what stills it ...
> This eye's zenith
> So only lit
> By your glory –
> Oh fill it all!

Robert's 1948 Christmas card for his beloved Margaret was also handmade. It is even more elaborately constructed; inside a stiff card cover, he had stitched four folded sheets of thinner paper, making a little booklet. On the front he glued a photo of Michelangelo's Creation of Adam, with his translation of lines from Rainer Maria Rilke copied underneath:

> I live my life in expanding rings,
> (as the circular waves in a pond,)
> which slowly reach out to all things.
> The last one perhaps I shall not fill,
> (I circle round God for thousands of years,)
> but attempt it I will.

There follows a lengthy love letter, alternating between his reflections on the spiritual life, using more quotations from Rilke, and his feelings for her:

> I sat down at my desk at ten o'clock last night with only
> one idea: to spend the night wholly with you. Margaret!

I wish to consecrate this night to you ... In that silence, Dearest, I found ever and again, I love you with all my being! Bless you this Christmastide, my love! May God grant me the power to make you happy this coming year. A sweet embrace from your Own.

Now I was learning about another Robert, an ardent and romantic soul. What lovers they were!

And how young they were ... The birthdays Robert described in these letters to his siblings were my mother's twentieth birthday, and his own twenty-first. Thinking of my own children at that age, they were students in further education and still dependent on their parental home and income; they didn't settle down with long-term partners for another decade. I can imagine that, for different reasons, each of my parents were looking to this youthful relationship to provide what they were missing. Margaret would have been seeking romance and adventure after a stultifying small-town childhood, and Robert, victim of so much loss and change, needed love and comfort and stability.

In September 1947, Robert wrote:

On Margaret's birthday we soon dropped our marvellous plans, and let reason (and the size of our purses) persuade us to have a pleasant and quiet time at home. So Friday night we travelled there by bus (how posh! We have always cycled up till now) and after supper and a walk, slept soundly until late morning.

The distance from Leicester to Ashbourne is over 40 miles, over hilly terrain. In their day, bicycles were heavy and had no gears, and yet this was apparently their usual mode of transport. It is interesting that he refers to the Kirklands' place in Ashbourne as 'home'. Perhaps his own family's London apartment did not feel like home after his mother had died. The market town of Ashbourne is of a similar size and status to Landshut, where they had last been a family before their diaspora. Perhaps, like me, he felt rootless, or perhaps he felt the draw of a conventional two-parent family, with a mother to fuss over him.

The next day, Robert wrote, he was up an hour earlier than their prearranged time to prepare a birthday table for Margaret, as was the custom in his family. This was to the great surprise of the Kirklands who had celebrated no birthdays since their daughter was fourteen, he claimed. I imagine him arranging flowers around her place setting, perhaps finding the best china from the top shelf in the pantry. This continental custom of a special birthday breakfast must have seemed so romantic to the Kirklands, used to the plain-living austerity of the post-war English midlands.

> Later in the morning, one of her schoolfriends dropped
> in accidentally, and we argued communism, atheism and
> many other isms ...

These kinds of conversations feel typical of my own growing-up in the 1960s but were not common in the Kirkland household – although perhaps my grandfather, Fred, may have listened with interest. A clever but deeply shy man, he had come home radicalised after his military service as a groom in the First World War. He wanted to support the growing labour movement, to form and join unions, but my more conventional grandmother, Mabel, was having none of it. The closest Fred got to his political dream was to become a member of the cooperative movement; he spent the rest of his working life behind the cheese counter in Mayfield village's Coop shop.

After lunch, Robert and Margaret took 'a long and glorious walk' to the lower reaches of the Dove. When they got home after dark, they found a house full of children (Margaret's cousins), 'eagerly awaiting our arrival (so that they might get on with the supper).' He appreciated that one of them, Pamela, 'a sweet kid of twelve [was] rather like Margaret, (or rather what she must have been like at that age)'. After the children went home at 10 o'clock, the two lovers went for yet another walk. He describes her hometown:

> Ashbourne lies very cosily in a little mould, with a solid core and spidery arms stretching along the six main roads; some of the houses are getting halfway up the hills, and it's a very pretty pattern at night.

I imagine he is comparing the hollow shape of the valley to a jelly mould.

The following day, Sunday, 'was a very lazy day indeed, with only a two-hour walk, and Mr Kirkland drove us to Leicester in the car', Robert wrote. Fred had a black Ford Popular; he had to double declutch when changing down through the gears, and lightly pump the brakes when descending Derbyshire's many steep hills. I remember being taken out in it as a child, feeling nauseous from the exhaust fumes in the slippery leather back seat. Granny squeaked softly in the front, pressing her hand to the dashboard in an alarmed effort to slow the car down. In those days, each small town had a different afternoon for their shops' half-day closing. On Wednesdays, Mayfield's half-day closing and Fred's afternoon off, it was my grandparents' custom to visit a neighbouring town for an excursion, finishing up with afternoon tea in a teashop. On those occasions when they invited me to join them, the car journey took from me any pleasure in these trips.

Five months later, in February 1948, Robert celebrated his coming of age. He wrote to Eva to thank her for her birthday present, a dressing gown:

> ... it's an absolute beaut and fits me very well (except that my slender waist is a good six inches higher; but it only needs altering the loops for the lovely cord.) When you spoke in your letter about careering about morning and night, I just could not fathom what you meant until the parcel arrived the next day. Now I can lounge about in warmth and comfort, and look jolly respectable.

It was difficult in those post-war years both to get and to maintain clothes. Before domestic central heating and electric drying machines were commonplace, qualities of warmth and weatherproofing were even more important in a fabric, hence worthy of mention in letters home:

> ... when I left camp on Thursday night in my birthday suit (not the original one, but the brown one the tailor had altered) and newly re-proofed coat, I was a sight worth looking at.

I wonder how long it had taken before these siblings addressed each other in such automatic and idiomatic English, instead of in their native German. The first event of Robert's birthday weekend was to listen to Margaret's rehearsal with the Bach choir. It occurs to me that may have been how they first met, as he would have taken every opportunity to attend classical music concerts, as would she. Supper followed at her lodgings, and as it was too late for them to travel to Ashbourne that night, he relates that Mrs Spencer

... actually put me up! (That's pretty good for the Spencers, who are not so free and easy with young folk of the opposite sex. Only a year ago Margaret was forbidden to bring me into the house at all. See what an educational value we must have!)

I am glad he saw their reluctance as due only to his being the opposite sex. Perhaps the fact that Robert was German or Jewish had something to do with their earlier ban? Whatever the case, his outgoing personality and warm sincerity had obviously won them over.

They spent the rest of his birthday weekend with Margaret's parents in Ashbourne:

Then we set off early Friday morning, and after lunch at home, started out among the Derbyshire hills.

On every possible occasion and whatever the weather, this intrepid pair lost no time in going out walking:

Nature had really provided me with a glorious birthday treat, and there was anything from six inches to four feet of snow out there ... On Saturday we took Margaret's twelve-year-old cousin Pamela with us, plus Rover [Margaret's dog], and we went for the whole day to Dovedale, through drifts and blocked roads, through icy blasts of wind that coated our clothes and faces and hair with mattings of ice, but the hills were even more glorious than in summer. After we had had lunch in a hayloft above a cowshed, to the accompaniment of a lovely vile reek, we had tea in the evening at the (locally) famous Pike House Farm, real farm butter, eggs, scones, etc., by a roaring fire. We walked home through beautiful country flooded with the brightest moonlight.

Pamela tells me she still remembers to this day the magnificence of the tea at Pike House Farm, which must have seemed even more special during post-war rationing.

Tissington 1947; Pamela, dog Rover

Robert referred to my grandmother formally as 'Mrs Kirkland' despite thinking of her house as 'home':

> Mrs Kirkland had knitted a lovely off-white pullover for me from real Welsh wool.

Margaret gave him Beethoven's Ninth Symphony on records. These would have been 78 rpm and were recorded onto nine discs with seventeen sides. He told his sister, Eva, that this edition was the same as her own and that Margaret said they were 'just to start my own collection!' Having experienced his way of celebrating Margaret's birthday, the Kirklands must have wanted to make his twenty-first birthday a special event for this motherless young man.

On Sunday, they 'just went for a walk'. They had intended to go youth hostelling in the Peak District for this February birthday celebration, like the previous Easter, but 'in order to give Margaret's mother peace of mind, we refrained from that enterprise.'

After that 'glorious' weekend, Robert returned to camp on Sunday night, as he had to be on duty on Monday morning at 3 a.m., which was not unusual. But he had one final part of his birthday still to come:

> ... yesterday I allowed myself a last treat, and listened to the actual performance by Margaret and the Bach choir in Leicester Cathedral – it was ever so exciting, with an announcement from London and the red-light flashing, and it went off very well indeed ... Now all that is over, and I am again submerged in work ... It is one of the strange beauties of life, that on all these occasions we always think and feel that it could not be more beautiful or happy, and yet each event seems to supersede the last one.

I feel fortunate to have such a full account of these important birthdays. It seems this young man had a gift for happiness, both in giving and in receiving. I search my mind to see if I can match birthday memories around my coming of age. Nothing like these bright, magical days wrung from post-war greyness occurs to me, though I adored the outfit I wore to my brother's eighteenth birthday party in 1968: a copper-brown velvet dress, with a fitted bodice and gathered skirt; a dull metal butterfly threaded onto leather thongs to make a belt that tied behind my waist; and brown leather high-heel boots with skaters' laces up to knee height. But there were no snowy tramps, farmhouse teas or classical concerts for me, such as marked my parents' emergence into adulthood.

8

FELDAFING, MARCH 2014

After our trip to Munich, we visit Feldafing, a charming lakeside Bavarian town. My grandparents, Richard and Edith, had married here on 27 March 1922, and it was to this town that Richard returned to live out the rest of his life in 1954. We find a self-catering apartment on the attic floor of a large family house. The owners show high trust as we troop up and down the stairs past their living accommodation.

In the photo album that my mother annotated, there are a few photos of my grandfather, Richard, and his carer, Anny, in the garden of a substantial villa. Anny, who had been the children's nursemaid until forced by Nazi decree to cease employment with non-Aryans, returned to work for Richard when he went back to Germany. By then he was a lonely, elderly widower whose children had become English, and had grown up and left home. I haven't been back to Feldafing since we visited the two of them when I was six, trundling across Europe on a sleeper train. Under the photos in the old family album, Margaret had written the house address. I long to see it again.

Armed with a town map from the tourist office, we set off on foot to find it. The road twists round to the left and goes through an underpass, which I am sure I remember. We begin counting off the house numbers once we reach the right street. The large, well-established gardens have been subdivided to allow for the addition of modern new-build houses, often dwarfing the original residence. Indeed, an untidy building site containing a huge concrete edifice, protected by a massive, barking guard dog, hides the house we seek. Exploring tentatively, we find a driveway, hardly noticeable from the road. We edge past the new dwelling, go round a corner – and there it is: Grandfather Richard's house.

I have photocopies of the pictures of Grandfather and Anny outside the house, to explain our interest, and with that boost to my confidence, I ring the doorbell. A kind-faced man, perhaps in his mid-forties, opens the door, looking unfazed by this strange group on his doorstep. Our son Eric, the best German speaker among us, begins to explain the reason for our visit, while I hold out the photocopied sheet, adding excuses in English. I have been here before, I add, in 1959, to visit my grandfather.

The man standing on his threshold takes one look and says, 'Of course. Come right in.' He then apologises for not being able to show us the entire house, as his son is sleeping upstairs. We hastily repudiate any desire to make a complete inspection and enter the main room downstairs. A green tiled stove, set into a corner of the room and rimmed on two sides by a wooden bench, catches my attention.

'Oh, I remember this! We sat here to warm ourselves after playing in the garden, my brother and I. We collected snails and made a park for them with stones, but they kept escaping.'

'So the stove was here in the '50s?'

'Yes – but it seemed much bigger then, and I'm sure the bench ran all the way around it.'

He smiles.

'I think the previous owners changed the layout of these downstairs rooms, then we did too. And of course, you were smaller then,' he adds.

His English is perfect, his helpfulness instinctive – this is today's Germany! And this is where my family came from, before we were forcibly deracinated.

Feldafing. Richard with Anni. '58

Feldafing '61.

Richard and Anny, Feldafing 1961

9

LOST CHILD; KENYA, 1955

Over half a century before this second visit to Feldafing, and just a year after my recovery from my blood transfusion, my young father left his little family in Cheshire. Following the Mau Mau revolt for independence from their British colonial masters, he set off on his own to work in a refugee camp in Kenya. It was 1955, and I was just two years old, before the age of my conscious memory.

My mother, brother and I joined Robert in Nairobi a year later. Throughout my childhood, my father's work for the Ministry of Overseas Development, and later for the United Nations Development Programme, took us on two- or three-year contracts to developing countries; we lived in various countries throughout Africa and the Americas. His remit was to set up social work organisations, and to train local people as probation officers and approved school staff. Robert's habitual saying was 'My job is to work myself out of a job,' as he helped former British colonies to develop as independent countries.

So, until I reached adulthood, I was an expat, what sociologist David Pollock terms a 'third culture kid' in his book of the same name. Our culture is what gives us the outward signals of shared identity, such as clothing, language, food and social behaviour, as well as our internalised beliefs and values. These expat third culture kids – TCKs, he calls them – are those who have spent a significant part of their childhood outside their parents' home culture because their parents live and work in a different country. This shifting between cultures takes place before TCKs have completed their childhood's developmental task of establishing their own identity and sense of belonging, and this dislocation can have lifelong consequences.

I feel a surge of recognition as I read Pollock's book. As he explains, TCKs' first culture is that of their parents' home or passport country (which may sometimes be more than one, in a mixed marriage). They call this place 'home', and perhaps visit for holidays to see their extended family, but they share no day-to-day experience with their contemporaries who live and go to school there. TCKs are like 'hidden immigrants'; they speak the home culture's language flawlessly and don't stand out as being foreign, but they have vastly different experiences and values – a different culture. When I first attended the little PNEU (Parents' National Education Union) school in Ashbourne during home leave at the age of seven, my fellow pupils couldn't believe my ignorance: 'You mean you don't know that's a blackbird? buttercup? conker?' Playtime delivered one humiliation after another.

The second culture of TCKs is the one of the country they are living in now, where they are incomers, perhaps transiently if their parents keep moving for their work. They do not belong here either, being ethnically different, and often having different social, financial, religious and cultural conditions to those they live among. Their school attendance is disrupted by periodic home leave, as well as curtailed by the next posting. I wasn't at the PNEU for more than a few months before returning to Ghana International School for another block of time.

And TCKs' third culture is that of others who share their own experience, that of repeated transitions, having full ownership of neither their first nor second cultures. Rather, research has shown, TCKs have the strongest sense of belonging with other TCKs, who are also part of this transient lifestyle. Many pupils of international schools are in this position. Before the internet made connecting a little easier, that very transience made it difficult to keep friends – there is only so far letter-writing can go to maintain a childhood accord.

Loss and separation, trauma and abandonment are common themes for TCKs. This can be compounded by being sent away from their parents to be educated in their home country, sometimes at a very young age. My brother, Mark, was ten when he was sent from Ghana to a boys' boarding school in England, and I was twelve when I went to the sister school. After our first permitted weekend outing with our parents, the hymn at evening assembly was Now Thank We All Our God; at the line 'Who from our mother's arms hath blessed us on our way', I began to cry and couldn't stop. Even today, decades later, my throat constricts when I remember those words and I find it difficult to speak them aloud in a normal voice.

The words of the spiritual song, 'Sometimes I feel like a motherless child, a long way from home,' still resonate with me.

The same cycle of emotions applies for coping with loss as with death: denial, anger, sadness, bargaining, acceptance. Any of these can be revisited throughout a person's life, when some chance event triggers a memory, evoking feelings of insecurity and instability: 'Where do I belong, where do I fit in? Who am I as a person?' These are the questions I find myself asking, even now, after what must seem from the outside to be a busy, fulfilling life with an established home, family and career.

John Denver was a TCK, the son of a military father. His classic song, Leaving on a Jet Plane, had great significance for me as a teenager when it first hit the charts. As the singer prepares for departure, he speaks about his deep loneliness, not knowing when he will be able to return to his lover. In a BBC Radio special programme, Denver said about the song:

> This is a very personal and very special song for me. It doesn't conjure up Boeing 707s or 747s for me as much as it does the simple scenes of leaving. Bags packed and standing by the front door, taxi pulling up in the early morning hours,

the sound of a door closing behind you, and the thought of leaving someone that you care for very much. I was fortunate to have Peter, Paul and Mary record it and have it become a hit, but it still strikes a lonely and anguished chord in me, because the separation still continues, although not so long and not so often nowadays.

And as for me, I remember running away from a group of teenage buddies to hide my tears, as one of them sang that song while he strummed his guitar. That was my life he was describing, and I couldn't talk about it, to anyone; I knew they couldn't understand.

Pollock writes that unrecognised and unresolved grief can lead to depression, to disproportionate anger, to closing oneself off in relationships. Especially where the parents are altruistically doing good in a poverty-stricken second culture, it is hard for their comparatively well-off children to express, or even understand, their own needs. I recognise this description. When I was twelve and newly delivered to boarding school, my mother tried to get me to befriend a Nigerian girl, whom I shall call Aina. I was to include her in any treats or excursions I was offered. She was a few years older than me, and I quickly found out that socialising across year groups was 'not done'. As an adult, I can now understand my mother's motivation – she must have known that Aina's family had been torn apart by the Nigerian Civil War, with their daughter placed in this English boarding school for her safety. Reading Adichie's *Half of a Yellow Sun* years later, Aina's beautiful, sad face sprang out at me from every page. Of course I should have comforted and befriended her. But I was told nothing of these horrors, perhaps being deemed too young to understand, and in any case, I was sunk into a shellshocked stasis of my own homesickness. I felt locked in, unable to reach out to anyone or to express my own need.

Whereas my mother, Margaret, had stayed in the same small town through her formative years, my father, Robert, had experienced this repeated uprooting too, as National Socialism bore down on German society. His family moved several times within Germany between 1933 and 1938, and then made the tremendous leap to their old enemy, England. He had had to live, socialise and learn through a new language in a foreign country. Survivors of a world war themselves, my parents may have seen moving around the globe not as a problem, but rather as a privilege, the thrills of international adventures a benefit of the hard-won peace.

Former US president Barack Obama describes his rootless, TCK childhood in *Dreams From My Father*, another book that resonated deeply with me. The child of a white American mother and a black Kenyan father, he grew up partly in Indonesia and partly in Hawaii. I don't know how many schools he attended, but I chalked up ten, always needing to begin again, to learn a fresh modus vivendi, to try to fit in.

Like many TCKs, I suffer from vicarious grief, tearing up at the sight of others' partings at airports, for example. I could not tell my parents about my homesickness and unhappiness at boarding school, supposing somehow that I had to protect them from the enormity of my emotions.

Many TCKs go into caring professions in an attempt to deal with and assuage others' pain. They become the helpers in a community, to whom others tell their problems, without developing the ability to share their own pain and ask for help themselves. As a small child, I was known in the family as 'chief sticker-upper', as I would back anyone getting the worst of an argument, irrespective of right or wrong. When I became a teacher, I worked in learning support, English for foreigners, and preschool special needs. Just as my refugee father had, and perhaps through a similar psychological drive, I busied myself trying to save others.

My husband, J, was another TCK, an expat child. He was born in New York, of English parents who, like Robert, worked for the United Nations. J spent part of his childhood in Beirut and then in Switzerland. We married straight after I finished my postgraduate degree in education and moved to Scotland. We have lived there ever since. I was determined to give our children a different childhood to the nomadic ones we had both had. They would stay in the same neighbourhood, go through their classes with the same cohort – they would *belong* in Orkney. I felt myself to be a member of this community too, part of the playgroup and school-gate sisterhood. My job as support teacher gave me further connections with schools and families across Orkney's archipelago, and my husband worked for the local authority. We felt accepted and embedded in Orkney life.

And yet, there was a large stone lodged at the core of my sense of self that I tried to avoid stumbling against by keeping busy. I felt at the whim of moods and emotions, without being able to understand or control them. I'd been told that Eva had been affected by episodes of schizophrenia throughout her life. Was mental instability my inheritance? I suffered from panic attacks, which found expression in intense fury if I felt abandoned in a place. My reaction, for instance, if I went into a shop and my husband moved away from the exact spot where I'd left him, was triggered by events long in the past.

'Where were you? Why did you go away?' I'd hiss.

'But I was just over there, at the bookshop window. I wasn't out of sight – if you'd looked you would have seen me ... '

Getting lost had dogged me since childhood. When I was five, we had gone on holiday from our home in Nairobi to Malindi beach, at the very start of its fame as a holiday resort.

Kenya – holiday at Malindi 1958; Margaret, Mark, author

We stayed in a beach hut with another family, and we children spent our days playing on the sands outside. After a long afternoon spent absorbed in play, I tried to go home but couldn't remember which was our hut among the row of similar buildings. I walked one way, looking for the identifying signpost outside it, and then turned and walked the other way. Soon I was completely lost. Whenever strangers passed me, I turned towards the sea so they wouldn't see I was crying. At last, two holidaying English women realised something was wrong.

'Are you lost, my dear?'

'I can't find our beach hut,' I said, sobbing.

'We'll come with you, poppet. This way, is it?' We walked back the way I had come.

'No, it's not here,' I said.

So we turned and walked back in the other direction, until at last they understood that I really couldn't identify the hut where we were staying. Evening was falling as they took me to their hotel, the first to be built on that strip, and phoned the District High Commissioner. He was in his dress kilt, a Scotsman celebrating Hogmanay, but left his house party to help reunite me with my frantically searching parents. They must have feared the worst; wild animals roamed the bush behind the coastal road.

Kenya – holiday at Malindi 1958; our beach hut, author

On other occasions, I would look up at rows of dusty vehicles in a carpark, having trailed after the wrong woman from the shop to a strange car, thinking I was following my mother.

If there is such a condition as geographic dyslexia, I have it. I have no locality bump, and need to repeat a route many, many times before I have learnt it. In our early years of marriage, J and I used to visit friends who lived in Angus for regular weekends of rural relaxation. We would drive our Morris Minor from Edinburgh, an easy two-hour journey along a familiar route. When it was my turn to take the wheel, I would call out at every junction, 'Which way here?', and J would patiently answer 'Left' or 'Right'. On one occasion he tried an experiment: 'I'm not going to tell you – just guess.' I panicked and complained vociferously, but he was adamant. It turned out that, at a subconscious level, I did indeed remember the way, and we arrived safely as always. But even after this proof, I still feel anxious and embarrassed on any journey where I am navigating. It compounds my feelings of loss and abandonment, making them raw and live again, each and every time I feel unsure of where I am in space.

For the most part, though, in those happy years of child-rearing in a small island community, I knew where I was, both socially and geographically. I kept my head down and soldiered on as best as I could. For a while, the questions of identity abated; being the busy mum of small children was enough to make me feel recognised as a person, by others and, most importantly, by myself. I may have been confused by my peripatetic past, but I could impose a stable structure on my present.

10

INVITATION TO LANDSHUT; APRIL 2014

It seems that the world is indeed conspiring to open up my family's history for me. Hans contacted the *Stolpersteine für Landshut* committee on my behalf, and I receive two wonderful emails: one from the chairperson and another from the vice chairperson. Konrad Haberberger first explains that they founded their association 'Against Forgetting' in January 2012 for laying *Stolpersteine*, stumbling stones, for all the victims of National Socialism in Landshut, who were deported and murdered, who had to flee from Germany or who had resisted the Nazis (*www.stolpersteine-landshut.de*).

> For your great-grandparents, Adolf and Cäcilie Hirsch, two stumbling stones were laid in the street at 55–57 Theaterstrasse on 2 October 2012.

So, there are already *Stolpersteine* for my family – and, I read on, they are proposing to lay five more. Two years before I know anything about this part of my family history, Landshut citizens have already acted 'against forgetting'.

Konrad also sends me photographs of each family member, of the department store *Kaufhaus Tietz* and of Villa Hirsch, my great-grandparents' mansion, copied from the city archives of Landshut. Cäcilie was always known as Cilly, he says. He also tells me he has privately purchased over thirty *Delphin-Verlag* books:

They are always offered on eBay and are often still in very good condition.

His deputy offers more details in a follow-up email:

My name is Franz Gervasoni, and I am a teacher at Hans-Carossa Grammar School ... My students and I have done a lot of research work in the Landshut archives. And it might be interesting for you to know that your uncle, Stefan Klaus Robert Landauer, and your father, Robert Felix Landauer, went to this grammar school in the middle of the thirties. (Your aunt, Eva Maria Landauer, went to a type of girls' junior high school for ages five to sixteen.) This is what my students and I found out when we worked on an exhibition titled 'A Part of Us – Tracing Back the Fates of the Jewish People of Landshut'.

The opening ceremony for this exhibition took place on 8 November 2013, which was the eve of the seventy-fifth anniversary of the so-called *Reichspogromnacht*, during which all the male Jews were arrested and taken to Dachau, but all of them were released a few days or a few weeks later. Some decided to leave Germany; others didn't and were taken to concentration camps in Poland where they were killed or died because of the appalling living conditions. Five of them died by suicide the night before being deported to Theresienstadt.

In the archives of our school, we came across some documents about your relatives – personal files for Stefan and Robert Landauer containing the school reports for both of them!

I remember from school history lessons that *Reichspogromnacht* is also known as *Kristallnacht*, the night of broken glass, as Nazis coordinated attacks on Jewish properties. 9 November was not long after the date, 19 September, when, according to Dr Schier, Richard had de-registered his family from the police record in order to move to London. So they had got away before that dreadful night, but my great-grandparents, Adolf and Cäcilie Hirsch, must have been caught up in it.

As I try to get my head around so much information, not even dreamt of hitherto, I read the closing sentence of Konrad's email again. He is inviting me to visit the stumbling stones.

I reply at once that I would very much like to see this memorial to my great-grandparents and I begin to set arrangements in place.

I try to reflect on what it might mean to actually see stumbling stones laid in memory of my great-grandparents. I had never met them, yet they were important citizens in pre-war Landshut. It feels a little abstract at this time. What catches my heart, however, is the possibility of learning more about my father as a schoolboy. I go back to his letters, searching for the man I knew as my father.

Robert's ardent nature, his energy and passion, can be seen in his religious belief as much as in his love life.

Following Stephen and Phyllis' Quaker wedding, Richard had been drawn into a discussion with his youngest son about the Friends' philosophy. Robert wrote:

> And then you go on to the question that really brings me onto my subject for tonight: '*Ob die Quaeker nicht nur die guten Taten, sondern auch disern [sic. for diesen], so zu sagen, atmosphärischen Wert betonen?*' (Whether the Quakers

emphasise not only the good deeds, but also value, so to speak, the atmosphere?)

It is interesting that, in these letters, Robert quoted his father's question, which had been posed in German, but then replied in English. He must have known Richard would understand the reply even if his father didn't initiate discussions in English. (While Robert and his older siblings thought of themselves as English, I was almost an adult before I discovered that, to non-family listeners, my father still had a German accent – I had no idea.) This question from Richard had triggered three pages of closely typed outpouring from Robert, of which I shall quote only a fraction. The tenor of this letter, written by a twenty-year-old to his sixty-five-year-old father, is strangely lecturing. Would Richard have been proud to think he had given this young lad such confidence as he made his way into adulthood? I hoped so.

Robert answered his father's question with 'an overwhelming 'Yes', and I hardly know where to start for the many thoughts that come crowding in'. He explained that 'good deeds' result from Quakers' inward attitude. Despite having no creed or dogma, Quakers hold definite beliefs, which are expressed by each in their own way.

> But with all that diversity of interpretation, one thing runs through all Quaker thought, and is the foundation of our belief, on which must rest all our actions and thinking: The guidance of the 'Inner Light', 'That of God within us', – or just plain God.

Robert claimed that social reform, in which Friends are 'well to the fore ... is one of the most vital results of their faith.' It is true that, for nearly four hundred years, Quakers have been known for taking action against slavery, war, racism and poverty. Still today, Quakers maintain that their purpose is to search for truth rather than to follow a creed or doctrine; they try to help each other discover how best to live out their faith within their community.

Robert went on to reflect on Jesus' importance, showing how deeply he had thought about his religion:

> ... it is my personal belief that Christ did not become a mediator between God and us – we have no need of that, for we can approach God ourselves, directly, so to speak ...

He thought that 'Jesus was like us, born the natural way, and living the normal life of a working lad brought up by religious Jewish parents in those days.' His impression of Jesus was of a man of high intelligence who took more than the usual interest in religion and the scriptures: '...as you will still find among thousands of young people nowadays.' It almost sounds as if Robert is describing himself with these words – as Eckhart Tolle said, we made god in our own image.

> And he was a rebel, even as young people today are rebels ...

Robert suggested that Jesus rebelled against the Old Testament idea of a vicious God of revenge who inspires fear, and against the myriad trivial traditional rules – that, for Jesus, God is love. The Old Testament was, of course, taken from the Jewish Bible; as we know, at some stage in the past, their branch of the Landauer family had relinquished their Jewish faith, converted to Catholicism and assimilated into German culture.

Robert then considered what happened to Jesus in the next thirty years. He assumed that he 'experienced life' and shared the sufferings of those around him, giving him both understanding and a love of them.

Jesus sinned during these years of young adulthood; the sins of a great man are not the sins of a little one, and the most grievous sin of a sensitive man would be imperceptible to a callous conscience. To a man who taught that the outward act was less significant than the inward attitude, inward despair concerning the existence of God would be far more terrible than any lawless living in which this despair should find its utterance ...

Adolescence is a time when we question what we have been taught, but Robert's depth of reflection seems to me exceptional for such a young man.

Robert continued by describing Jesus' teaching about the Kingdom of God, which he said can be understood in two ways: the first is the eventual reign of God on earth –

an idea which had been part of the Jewish religion for a long time, but, as before, I am not very interested in that

– and the second is a state of godliness within the individual, as Jesus had achieved. He wrote this letter to his father on the fifth anniversary of his mother Edith's death. He finishes:

I do not think that man can accomplish this happy state so completely as Jesus did – but I know [one] who came very near to it: ...Mother, whose essential being was happiness, love and peace.

He was truly her son.

If Robert was his mother's son in the sense of inheriting her warm faith, I ask myself, am I his daughter in the same way? Despite having been brought up as a Quaker and attending a Quaker boarding school for four years, I have no belief in any god. The term 'atheist' positions itself around considering the existence of a god and hence I reject it. I find the rhetoric of religion tedious, and I see that historical actions carried out in the name of various religions deliver as much violence and cruelty as good. On the other hand, I love the beautiful language and musicality of the King James Bible and of much church music. Some of the more unusual offerings in *Songs of Praise* were staples of my Quaker boarding school: Emily Brontë's haunting No Coward Soul is Mine ('There is not room for death, nor atom that his might could render void'), or the socialist When Through the Whirl of Wheels and Engines Humming ('God in a workman's jacket'), and When Wilt Thou Save the People? ('Not thrones and crowns, but men!'). I am drawn to elements of many belief systems, such as Buddhism and Druidism. I also espouse the moral and ethical underpinnings of Quakerism but feel no need for 'faith' or 'worship'. Of course, I wish now I had had such conversations with my father. The nearest we came was a discussion about different sects in Christianity, where he smiled ruefully as he said that my mother was slipping back into the Church of England of her upbringing. I hope I have at least inherited his good-humoured tolerance.

Robert's youthful habit of positive thinking fitted well with the *zeitgeist* in psychology in the middle of the last century. Psychologists had previously studied maladaptive behaviours following a medical model of alleviating or curing illness. Some began to believe that whatever you focus your attention on grows, so there arose 'positive psychology', a movement to study instead what leads humans to happiness and wellbeing. The idea is to find out 'what works' when building beneficial character traits and experiences, so as to do more of it. Altruism, the capacity to put the wellbeing of others before one's own, is developed throughout childhood. It is affected by internal, or personality, factors – empathy, optimism, a sense of justice – as well as by social factors, such as family, culture and experience. Robert's sunny nature, his family's appreciation of their little *Floh*, and the loving example of both his mother, Edith, and his grandmother, Cilly, counteracted the many griefs his family experienced.

He wrote to Stephen and Phyllis:

> Whatever may happen, I am full of confidence and that *joie de vivre* you mention, and very happy. In some ways I am sorry that I have not more time to live this life more fully and less hastily, and yet what more could I wish than to work for those who have been denied that full and happy life. I hope I shall soon be allowed to do that, and in that work and my private life find satisfaction and happiness and joy.

This summarises his motivation for the social work career he was aiming for: an altruistic desire to help those less fortunate than himself. To an objective eye, his life story seems to be one of repeated loss and trauma. Perhaps it is a coping mechanism, to see the glass as half full rather than half empty. And yet, more than that, Robert's glass seems to brim over.

His efforts to express his world view, both his own awareness of happiness and his desire to care for others, led to this almost incoherent tumbling out of words:

> Perhaps it's nothing so extraordinary, but I always feel that we four have been and are very fortunate, in that we find happiness and joy in our lives, despite not very congenial circumstances and a very dreary outlook onto the world at large – mainly because of our attitude to life which allows us to be personally happy while yet deeply feeling with

people and the world in their misery, an attitude which allows us to laugh at ourselves, and the pathos and bathos around us, without which humour, life must be a heavy burden instead of a source of joy in this twentieth century.

His phrase 'we four' referred to the recipients of the letter, Stephen and Phyllis, and to Margaret and himself. At that stage, they were a congenial foursome and nicknamed themselves 'Stephyl' (Stephen and Phyllis) and 'Roma' (Robert and Margaret). It is interesting that Robert assumes the other three mirror his feelings, and yet we have evidence that Stephen, at least, had a very different personality to that of his younger brother.

Stefan (Stephen) had been bullied at the Hans-Carossa Grammar School, and again in England. Bullying can be defined as the mistreatment, whether physical, verbal or exclusionary, by the powerful towards those who are weaker or different in some way. Any signs of anxiety or low self-worth are quickly exploited. I too was bullied at stages throughout my life. I coped by bribing at age six in London ('Do you still play with that car I gave you?'), and by standing up to the bully at age eight in Ghana ('Ok then, just do it!' – my terror made me want to just get it over with). In both instances, boys were making physical threats to me. I don't think these episodes were particularly damaging in the long term; I acted, and the problem was resolved. But I had no resources to cope with the chronic verbal and psychological bullying at girls' boarding school. There was literally no escape, day after night, night after day, through each long term. This experience has cast a long shadow through the years, leaving me unable to cope effectively with bullying in those few instances when it occurred in my adult, professional life. If only I had been able to ask for help as a teenager. My father might have known what to do, I now realise, and perhaps could have given me tools for the future.

As Robert was growing into adulthood, he showed that he was thinking deeply about wrongdoing and reparation, with empathy for those who had fallen into wrongdoing. He describes having to act as an escort to a girl of nineteen, only a year younger than himself, who had been found in the Scraptoft POW camp. The police wanted her for theft, larceny and, with two men, armed robbery. He was quick to see the best in her:

> I felt really sorry for the kid, who had been used to that kind of life for some five years, and although unable to settle down in a job for more than a few months, was quite a decent, clean and cheerful girl.

I wonder whether he thought of the POWs he was working with as a malevolent enemy who had caused his family to flee from everything they had known. Or did he see them as ordinary people, not unlike himself, caught up in a war machine not of their volition? Because of my belief that the war was long past, of little relevance for our family as I was growing up, I didn't ask him these questions during his life. I believe, though, that his lifelong adherence to the principles of rehabilitation and education, of reparation rather than punishment, had its roots in this formative experience. He complains to Stephen and Phyllis that proposed reforms to the penal code 'don't go far enough, still have too much accent on punishment, instead of restitution and help for the individual. – However, we can talk about all that.'

These letters seem to be extensions of the kinds of conversations Robert habitually had with his friends and family. I feel a fresh rush of love for this ardent young man, who was a living example of positive psychology – and who, a mere five years later, was to become my father. I can learn from his example. It's not too late. Perhaps visiting Landshut, his home through those critical years of a child's development between five and ten, will throw further light on who my father was.

11

ROBERT'S EARLY ADULTHOOD; LETTERS, 1947 – 1950

The Landauers were not brought up in the Jewish faith and my father's youthful 'conversion' was from Catholicism to Quakerism. I wonder, though, what my father and his siblings felt about their Jewish blood – or perhaps they felt wholly German, in terms of race. They were certainly very keen to become English and were naturalised as soon as they could be. Robert wrote,

> As soon as I have paid £10, I'll have become a British citizen. My demob. may now take place.

I have seen my father's naturalisation certificate, signed on 15 March 1948; this entitled him to 'all political and other rights, powers and privileges' and made him subject to 'all obligations, duties and liabilities, to which a natural-born British subject is entitled or subject …'

Having now achieved this ardently desired goal, and following his demobilisation, the summer of 1948 spent cherry-picking was a time of limbo for Robert, as he waited to hear the outcome of his efforts to secure his future. He had applied to the London School of Economics to study to become a social worker. The work he had done with German prisoners of war led to his growing interest in crime and punishment, rehabilitation and restitution, as evidenced in his letters.

In November 1947, though, he had still been unsure of exactly what route to take, and how to finance it:

... I want to know whether to apply for a grant and for which course, also whether to apply for a Youth Leadership course before going to LSE.

Yet again, however, he looked for the silver lining:

... somehow I am feeling very optimistic lately, and am truly glad that I am getting to the end of my period of service. Quite apart from the right or wrong of the case, I don't think the time was all wasted, and I feel that with the experience gained and greater maturity, I can start afresh on work of my own choosing – perhaps it was necessary for me to be slightly older before I could start seriously in my job.

He experienced disappointments too. None of the summer jobs he had hoped for worked out, as he explained in January 1948:

I heard last week from the National Association of Boys' Clubs that they are not running their usual summer course (as they themselves told me in November they would, when I went there with Eva), so that I hope to take up some (preferably paid) job which will give me a look in on social work, and do perhaps part-time help in a youth club.

He also considered other forms of paid employment, but was perhaps tired of being defined, career-wise, by his German background:

I don't know whether I'd be acceptable, but something along the lines of an advert. in this week's New Statesman: 'Responsible trained Secretary, under 45, required for interesting case work, knowledge of German desirable.

Salary according to qualifications.' Three things about that particular one: from my point of view, it sounds good, except that it smells a bit of refugee work, which I don't want (I want normal British conditions), but otherwise casework gives me an excellent look into the workings of many types of social work, the best preview I could have without training. But from their point of view, am I trained? I think so, after all this office-squatting experience; and another snag, I can only take it for a maximum of six months. But anyway, that's the sort of thing I'm thinking of. – As you see, I'm already planning ahead, and am not at all downhearted about my first defeat.

'I want normal British conditions' – Robert did not want to be any different from the Englishmen among whom he lived and worked, but, of course, he was. He was still a German Jewish refugee, albeit on the cusp of naturalisation as a British subject. His name was still the Germanic Landauer. When he and Margaret married on 6 August 1949, the certificate was made out in the name of Robert Felix Landauer. It was not anglicised to Landor until the following year, just a few months before the birth of their first child, my brother Mark.

Eventually Robert heard that the London School of Economics had taken up his three references. Although that looked hopeful, he continued to apply to other universities' social work courses, as a fallback. It strikes me now that he made his own good luck, through actively searching for opportunities and through cheerful perseverance. The 2020 film Limbo follows a group of four refugees, each from a different country and with English as their only common language. They have been housed on a fictional remote Scottish island while they wait for the results of their asylum claims. The landscape is bleak, and despite some comedic moments, feelings of grim hopelessness, of endlessly waiting in limbo, pervade the story. Why does my father's narrative feel so different? To be sure, the political context has completely changed over the intervening eighty years, but I think it is also that he displayed an energetic agency wherever it was possible. He remained positive even when he had no control over events.

After my mother's death, we found a framed card in a drawer. The text, written out in my father's distinctive handwriting, read: '...grant me the serenity to accept the things I cannot change, courage to change the things I can, and wisdom to know the difference.' It is known as Niebuhr's Serenity Prayer, and it seems to me that this young man, my future father, embodied it.

Robert was forced to leave his birth culture; Margaret chose to leave hers. Pamela's account of my parents' wedding in 1949 demonstrates the difference between the customs of the community Margaret had grown up in and those of her new life. Pamela explained that the Kirklands and the rest of the extended family were members of Ashbourne's main Protestant church, St Oswald's. Fred Kirkland, father of the bride, was a sidesman for St Oswald's; this is an assistant churchwarden, responsible for taking the collection, welcoming and ushering the congregation, and overseeing all arrangements such as seating. Mabel, mother of the bride, was a lifelong member of St Oswald's Mothers' Union, knitting, sewing and fundraising for good causes. They must have looked forward to the day their only child would walk up the aisle to be married, supported by the community of the church where they had raised her. Instead, Fred ordered a large taxi to transport them all to the Friends Meeting House in Leicester. On the way, they collected her Auntie Rebie, another of my grandmother's sisters, from her home in Osmaston village. Rebie had prepared buttonhole posies for each of them – pale pink carnations with small white flowers. The bride's family had all dressed up in their best as they would for a wedding at St Oswald's.

When they arrived in Leicester, they found a small, plain building, so different from Ashbourne's landmark edifice, their church. Robert had already experienced a Quaker wedding when Stephen and Phyllis were married three years previously, but for the Kirklands and their family, this seemed very strange. Once through the vestibule, the meeting room had its seats set out in a square, so the family sat looking round at the other members of the 'congregation'. In church they would all have faced the vicar, in rows of high-backed wooden pews. They saw that everyone else was dressed plainly, and Pamela wrote that she felt overdressed and very self-conscious of her buttonhole.

She described Margaret's wedding dress as bronze shot silk taffeta worn with bronze kid court shoes. The bride also wore a gold medallion on a pale green velvet ribbon, which had 'some significance for Robert from his earlier life', perhaps something that had belonged to his dead mother Edith – again, very different from the long white dress, train and veil traditional at church weddings. Pamela is still the most carefully dressed woman I know, always neatly and prettily turned out. I realise from this description that she must have always taken a knowledgeable interest in the quality and design of apparel.

A Friend stood up and said that they could see there were people present unfamiliar with their ways. He told them that the bride and groom would sit and consider, and that when they felt ready, they would make their vows to each other. Pamela wrote,

> I seem to remember that a long time elapsed before Robert,
> turning to Margaret, said words similar to those we all use
> in weddings, and then Margaret made a similar response.

Other Friends then stood and read a poem or piece of prose.

Robert and Margaret, wedding, Friends' Meeting House,
Leicester; 6 August 1949

I remember thinking in a worried way – had we all got to do this?

Her Uncle Will, my grandmother's only brother, winked at her – perhaps her anxiety had been evident.

In recent years, I have got to know Pamela better. She is now the last one of my parents' generation. We have another bond, too – we both have an adored gay son. Our son told us he was gay the summer after he left school. Whenever I shared the story of his coming out, I spoke of my mother's letter which assured him of her unchanging love, and described the importance to us all of this warm acceptance. Then, just a few years ago, I stopped myself in my tracks. Margaret had died a full year earlier. There was no way she could have written him this wonderful letter – she was already dead. But I also knew that she would have done. That would have been her response. They say that your relationship with a person can continue to develop even after they have died. Margaret hasn't been in my life physically for over two decades, but I feel the truth of this assertion. I am continuing to pick at and loosen the complicated knots which snarled our connection, and to appreciate and honour my mother.

The newly married couple honeymooned in the Scilly Isles. Robert was in his element, sailing them in a borrowed dinghy. Midlander Margaret felt so seasick, she told me in later years, that she asked herself 'What monster have I married?' They stayed in a guest house, sharing the breakfast room with an elderly couple. Every morning the wife asked her husband, 'Sugar in your tea, dear?' and every morning the husband replied gently, 'You know I never take sugar in my tea, dear.' Margaret observed this example of a long marriage with dread, she used to joke. How sad that my parents never had the chance to grow old together, and to see for themselves how it was.

Robert and Margaret lived in London with Richard at the start of their marriage. Pamela told me of a trip to London soon after her older cousin's wedding; her parents, Nan and Ernest Smith, wanted to attend the November remembrance service in the Royal Albert Hall. Newly-wed Robert and Margaret took Pamela to an Ice Spectacular in the lavish Renaissance-style Stoll Theatre, sitting high in the gods.

Robert was completing his studies at the London School of Economics and Margaret had her first teaching job. She fell pregnant very soon, which was unintended. (When I was experiencing nausea in pregnancy, she told me about her own, which was triggered by

Richard's German method of making coffee in a covered jug. He left this steeping all day in a simmering pan of water, giving off a burnt, bitter smell that lingered throughout the flat. Strong continental coffee would not have been familiar in the Kirkland household, where tea or milk-based drinks were the only hot beverages taken.) Before my brother Mark was born, our parents moved to the village of Kerridge in Cheshire. They lived in Bobbin Cottage, whose garden backed onto the canal, and Robert began his career as a probation officer.

On 25 September 1950, a week after my brother's birth, Robert wrote to Stephen and Phyllis, telling of their progress; he hoped that Margaret and the baby would be home by the following weekend. It was normal in those days to spend longer in the maternity hospital than is the case now. He wrote about their options for a twenty-first birthday present for her, as her coming of age was nine days after she gave birth. Everything on her wish list was for her new life as housewife and mother. Included are a few objects of beauty – walnut table utensils, coloured glassware, bright blue bulb dish – but most are practical requirements: kitchen scissors and knives, cake tin, garden shears and secateurs, kitchen scales. That last item had to weigh up to thirty pounds for the baby and down to one ounce for baking, 'not spring balance'.

Robert explained their choice of names for their son:

> ...the first we have had in mind for very long, the second not quite so long, but apart from its obvious meaning, we also like it for its association with Christmas, when he was conceived.

It is clear that referring to a child's conception when naming it is not just a contemporary phenomenon; I suppose my brother should be thankful he wasn't called Finchley or Goldhurst.

Robert concludes touchingly:

> Let me introduce to his aunts and uncle (he has so very few!)
> Mark Christian Landor.

Indeed, there were so very few of the Landauer family left to welcome the next generation.

12

SCATTERED PIECES; SWITZERLAND, APRIL 2014

I feel immense gratitude to Hans for having taken so much trouble for a stranger. He engaged with me at a chance social meeting, then researched my father's family and forged links with relevant people and organisations in Germany on my behalf. I would not have known where to begin to seek any of this information for myself. I write to ask if he would be interested in visiting the *Stolpersteine* with us. I explain that, without his help, none of this would have come about, and perhaps he might enjoy witnessing the fruit of his labour.

His reply shows he is well ahead of me in foreseeing possible repercussions:

> Thank you for your description of what you have planned for your trip into history. I'm sure you understand better than I what an emotional impact this will have on you ... The chain of stories told from one generation to the next is at the heart of our culture. In your family, it has been badly broken by what Germans have done to your ancestors. Picking up the scattered pieces and dangling ends of this story, you will reconstruct a few of the lost links – and that ushers in astonishingly intense sentiments. I remember how, for several weeks, after visiting my grandfather's grave and having read some of the preserved documents, I had the feeling he was looking over my shoulder when I was at work.

Therefore, even if it wasn't so far a journey, I would much rather leave this delicate journey to you, J and your family. We will most certainly stay in contact and, once you are able to, you will tell me how it went.

If Hans is right, the forthcoming trip to Landshut may be more traumatic than I realise. I feel grateful that he is still willing to remain part of my journey into my family's past. But I dismiss his warning, feeling secure in my bubble of ignorance; the past is finished, nothing to do with the me of today ...

Then I think back to the early 1940s, when Robert and his family were newly living in a foreign land. Stefan and Robert experienced ugly name-calling in the streets. During term time they were sent to boarding school, a not uncommon custom in England, but one unfamiliar to them. Today there is much research into 'boarding school syndrome', exploring the potential damage done to a child's emotional and social development. This can have a lifelong impact on the adult personality, giving 'survivors' a deep need for power and control, and an incapacity for empathy and connection. Joy Schaverien in *Boarding School Syndrome: the Psychological Trauma of the 'Privileged' Child* describes an ABCD of abandonment, bereavement, captivity and dissociation. Siblings who share boarding school experience can form a closer bond than usual, as I did with my brother. I recognise, in myself and in others, those recurring memories: of having been left for months at a time; of having no escape from tormentors; of the homesickness that is like a bereavement; and of the polite, determinedly positive relationship you maintain with your parents, because you can't allow any true feelings to escape. To this day, packing for a trip evokes severe anxiety: will I have everything I need? At boarding school in those days, there was no way of remedying any lack. Teenage rebellion is too risky when you only see your parents once or twice a year, and in my case, those feelings of challenge only surfaced when I was an adult.

The English custom of sending very young children away from home exacerbates these effects, as 'preparatory school' starts at age eight for the 'privileged' class. Many features, such as spartan fare and unheated dormitories, would have been the same for Stefan and Robert as it was for my generation. Of course, with a war on, there would perhaps not have been the same differential in material comfort to their home life at that time, but separation from home and parents for these recently displaced children must have been traumatic. I wonder, too, if the custom of an initiation ceremony was the same for them as it was for us. My brother had all the bedroom furniture piled onto his bed with instructions not to move on his first night in boarding school. I was terrified by the threat of being made to jump off the bridge into the River Ouse with the whole school watching; my innocent gullibility made me easy prey. I imagine Stefan, with his serious sensitivity, being a similar target, but perhaps my irrepressible father, the Felix *Floh*, had laughed it off – 'Come on now, you're not serious!' Who knows?

By the time they came to England, Eva was too old for school and had no friends in London, with no means of meeting anyone new of her own age. Added to her probable anxiety over her safety and her future, she must have felt great loneliness.

At around this time, an American psychologist called Abraham Maslow was forming a developmental theory of human motivation. In this model, he proposes that human needs are hierarchical, with higher levels only attempted when each basic need has been met. Hence, the physiological requirements for survival – food, shelter, warmth – must be met first, before one can attend to the need for safety. This is followed, in order, by the need for a sense of love and belonging, for esteem, cognitive needs, aesthetic needs, self-actualisation (achievement of one's own goals), and finally for spiritual transcendence. Eva would have spent her years in Munich and Landshut fulfilling those higher levels of human motivation. These were exemplified by her excellent performance at the piano, her Catholic education leading to a lifelong friendship, and her exposure to the best in modern art through her father's life work. The Landauers had succeeded in fleeing the Nazis to come to a free London. Then war had broken out, and once again she had to focus all her attention on the most basic needs for survival and safety. Blacked-out streets, burning buildings and nightly bombing raids became the daily experience of Londoners. It may not have seemed to her to be much improvement from the life they had left in Germany.

Eva was the only woman from my father's family whom I had been able to get to know. After their widowed father Richard had returned to Bavaria in 1954, she lived alone in the family flat in Goldhurst Terrace. This was near the Finchley Road in Swiss Cottage – or *Finchleystrasse*, as it was dubbed, because of the high number of German refugees living in the area. At the end of Robert's three-year post in Nairobi, we had come to London, where he found work as a probation officer and Margaret worked as a teacher in a girls' secondary school. Having nowhere else to go, we lived with Eva. The family's ownership of a two-floor apartment had by then been reduced to a single-floor flat, with only two bedrooms, so our parents made up a bed every night in the sitting room. Mark and I shared the second bedroom. The rug between our two single beds became an island. This was the only way to cross the wild ocean that separated us, unless we climbed over the top of the wardrobe at one end of the room or inched along the windowsill at the other. Every morning thuds and crashes, fighting and crying disturbed our parents sleeping in the next room, and probably Eva too. Travel formed a thread in our childhood play as in life.

Our fear of African wildlife transmuted into a more domestic terror. When the bath's hot-water tap was turned on, the elderly gas geyser on the wall groaned and popped, and we knew that we could be gassed and die if the flame failed to reignite. We were still innocent of the knowledge of the Nazi gas chambers, but the adults weren't, and maybe transmitted something of their fear.

Getting lost was another feature of our London life. Unlike in Nairobi, where we were always accompanied by an adult, we now walked home from school on our own. We had been taught to turn off the main street at a particular hoarding – until one day it had been pasted over with a new advertisement, and we walked straight on. A passing woman saw our predicament and brought us safely home.

I hadn't yet learnt the skill of making friends and was easy prey for the class bully. Rather resourcefully, I told my mother we all had to bring a present for his birthday, and I presented the boy with a Dinky toy car the next day. Every time he came near me, I would remind him about the car I gave him. That was shameful, I know, but it worked.

A few doors down from Eva's flat was Ackermans, the famous chocolatier, where we spent our pocket money every Saturday. They had an affordable line of foil-wrapped chocolate pieces – pencils, cigars, sardines – and my favourite treat, praline babies swaddled in crunchy shells of pink or blue blanket. We visited our younger cousins in Blackheath, Stephen and Phyllis' children, and were shocked to discover they got chocolate at bedtime – their teeth! – as well as thrilled to try out their heavy lawn roller, not something we'd ever needed in Nairobi.

For those few months, we could belong, with extended family members and neighbours who were also part of the German Jewish diaspora. We were part of a larger family, with aunts, an uncle, cousins.

Then we left, for Robert accepted a post in newly independent Ghana. Stephen's family left for Sierra Leone a few years later, leaving Eva to live alone for the rest of her life. I wonder now why these young men, once so jubilant to achieve their English naturalisation, felt drawn to make their careers abroad. Were they aware that they were unwittingly falling into the trope of the mythical Wandering Jew, who was cursed to walk the earth in perpetuity for having mocked Jesus on his way to the cross? Perhaps they were finding that, despite their English schooling and national service, they weren't quite British, although they were no longer German. It may have felt easier to be accepted among other international expats, other third culture dwellers.

Grandparents' garden, Ashbourne 1960; Fred, Mabel, Robert, Margaret, Mark, author

A year after our stay with Eva in the London family flat, my mother took my brother Mark and me to Ashbourne to stay with her parents, while we were on an extended home leave. My father had remained in Accra, working, and was to join us later. We had barely arrived when my mother left us with her parents, Fred and Mabel, and departed for

London. We weren't told very much, except that Eva was ill and she needed someone with her.

Except for my hospital stays as an infant, we had never been separated from our mother, and at first we found it hard. Granny and Grandad had their habits formed during their working-class war-time years, and still kept to the same rigid routine. Monday was always washday, and the twin-tub and mangle took over the kitchen. Granny would have already made the leftovers from the small Sunday joint into another dish for Monday's dinner, some version of shepherd's pie.

Dovedale stepping stones, Derbyshire 1960; Fred, Margaret, Mark, author

They always ate the main meal of the day, meat and two veg plus pudding, at twelve noon. There was porridge for breakfast, cocoa or molasses at elevenses, afternoon tea of garden-grown salad, bread, jam and 'everyday' cake, and supper of cream crackers and Milo, Horlicks or Ovaltine before bed. This routine felt so strange to us coming from Africa; there I always felt too nauseous from the humid heat to eat much at a mealtime, preferring a sweet and juicy snack, such as mango, pawpaw or guava. Granny pressed us to eat far more, and far more often, than I was used to. The food was stodgy with over-cooked sour-tasting vegetables, and her perpetual exhortations to eat distressed me. Also, we missed our mother; no-one could tell us when she would return.

In later years I learnt what had taken her to London for so long: Eva was suffering a breakdown in her mental health, and schizophrenia was named as the cause.

By then, Eva was a pharmacist in one of the big London hospitals, and clearly had been able to hold down this responsible job. (Through my adolescence, I was aware of my mother regarding me somewhat anxiously if I was in a low mood; she was hoping, she said, I hadn't inherited Eva's mental instability. This had the inevitable effect of making me more anxious, not less.) Eva continued to have episodes of schizophrenia, as we understood it then, throughout her life.

Robert had referred to 'Father's treatment of Eva' in a 1948 letter to Stephen. We can only guess what went wrong between them, but a few months earlier, in November 1947, he had written to Stephen and Phyllis:

> I'm glad she is seeing plenty of Alan, whom I've not had a chance to get to know as yet.

Phyllis explained to me a few years ago that Alan was a young curate and that he and Eva had been engaged to be married. She said they suited each other very well and spent hours playing piano duets together. Everyone who met him liked him. Alan was going to Africa as a missionary but somehow Eva did not go with him; she could not leave her father, whether through Richard's edict or Eva's conscience, it is now impossible to know.

A few months later Eva fled to the States, perhaps as the result of the first of her mental health breakdowns, which continued to dog her throughout her life. Robert refers to 'your sailing date' in a loving letter to her, written a week after his twenty-first birthday in February 1948:

> ... we are both going on a journey into a new land, a place we may have heard about before but have no knowledge of, taking new chances, shouldering new responsibilities, but on the whole taking much of the old along with us ...

He explained that he was comparing his coming of age, but even more his leaving the army, with Eva's journey to America:

> And so first of all, I want to wish you all the very best – for the journey, on which I do hope you won't feel the inclination to feed the fishes too strongly, and especially for your stay with Ted and Dora – I do hope those months will be really a holiday, recuperative and restoring after these last months, last years I could say.

Robert seems to be referring carefully to her low mood – 'inclination to feed the fishes' – whilst trying not to make too much of it. And it is interesting that Robert's first cousin Dora, and her publisher husband Ted Schocken, who looked after Mark and me some twenty years later, were already taking care of members of our family.

He finishes his letter with a jocular flourish to make her smile:

> Lots of love from your now big brother Robert. P.S. when do I get my promotion from *Floh* (flea) to the next higher rank – something like grasshopper, I suppose?

Among the pack of letters sent to me by Karen are several from Eva's American friends, warmly describing their homes and families and inviting her to come and stay with them. I assume these young women had been asked by Dora to offer friendship and hospitality to Eva, as I can't imagine how she would otherwise have had any opportunity to get to know them. The tone of the writing was hospitable but not very personal; these friends did not sound as if they were close connections like Erika Stadler. The writers offered exactly what she no doubt needed – pleasure excursions and undemanding company.

There was also one that had been forwarded to Eva at the Schockens' address in Scarsdale, New York, from a Miss Vane applying for the post of housekeeper for Richard:

Madam,

I send the following particulars for your kind consideration with reference to your advertisement in 'The Lady'.

I am a well-educated, well-read, well-travelled gentlewoman, of good family, tall, of good presence and pleasant personality, aged forty-eight, and experienced both as resident private secretary and as lady housekeeper. I am exceptionally tidy and methodical and keenly appreciative of quiet home life. I am accustomed to having the responsibility of a home, housekeeping, shopping, accounts, etc., but have only a slight knowledge of cooking.

I am free now and could call upon you any time at your convenience when I could give you full details regarding my experience, references, etc. I can truthfully say that I am most conscientious, loyal, and thoroughly trustworthy and reliable.

Yours truly,
Hilda E. Vane (Miss)
Reference: Lady Alice Warington.

I am moved by this glimpse into their lives, for several reasons. First is the fact that, even as Eva fled across the world to escape her father's difficult behaviour towards her, she still had his wellbeing at heart and had sought a housekeeper to look after him in her absence. And then there is what we can guess from Miss Vane's letter. Perhaps Hilda Vane had been in a similar position to Eva, an unmarried adult daughter caring for an elderly parent; unlike Eva, she must have had no professional training to fall back on after, I assume, her parents' demise. All she could offer were the cultural, social and caring skills of a 'lady'. The letter could have come from the pages of a Jane Austen novel. Thankfully, my Aunt Eva's family had supported her to have a career outside the home.

Another letter was from the matron at the hospital where Eva worked, envying her the proposed trip. The fact that from a lifetime's correspondence she preserved these letters speaks of their importance to her.

Writing to Stephen, Robert referred to their father's hurt at his letters to Eva being returned to him. Perhaps she did not feel emotionally able to cope with his demands, and even the sight of his handwriting triggered trauma for her. The various friends whom she was visiting would surely have forwarded any family letters to her, so it is likely that she herself instructed the return of his letters.

I can find no evidence as to what had happened between Richard and Eva, just these few hints from Robert's letters. I cannot now know what 'Father's treatment of Eva' amounted to – this troubled and troublesome man, a Victorian disciplinarian, who had lost everything he held dear – but to her and to her brothers it seemed abusive. It was one more trauma in Eva's life, which had started in gracious *Elisabethstrasse* as a beautiful, popular girl, and had ended so sadly.

Eva at Ursuline convent school, seated in armchair front right

War visits death and destruction and terror on those in the direct line of attack; its ripples spread outwards to touch everyone else, too. Life's expected pathways are torn up and families can burst apart under the strain. If only Edith hadn't died ... Eva had lost the protective love of both her mother and Cilly, her grandmother. I was fortunate to have had my maternal grandmother and my mother in my life until I was in my thirties and forties, and I am part of the lives of my daughter and little granddaughters. I am beginning to understand the importance of female nurturing, and to see my place in the chain of generations.

13

SENSE AND UNDERSTANDING; REFLECTION

Eva, Stefan and Robert grew up in the same household until they left Germany in 1938, attending day schools and returning home to their parents every afternoon. Even so, their experiences of childhood differed; they had left their home in *Elisabethstrasse*, Munich, at different ages. Eva was ten, Stefan eight and Robert only six. A child's consciousness and understanding differ between these ages.

A six-year-old is coming to the end of what in most countries is the preschool period. They are just beginning to form genuine friendships, and to understand that an event may appear differently when seen from another person's perspective. Cooperative play and make-believe play are strengthening. Robert would have been about to embark on formal education.

By the time a child is ten, as Eva was, their understanding has changed; they have a much better grasp of both emotional language and emotional self-regulation. Older children see that rule-following is part of a nuanced social and moral code, where context affects how an action is judged, whereas a younger child operates within black-and-white thinking, swinging between the two poles of punishment and reward.

These three Landauer children would have understood what was happening around them in very different ways, as they were forced from their home to seek shelter with their grandparents.

And how much greater is this phenomenon – different childhoods within one family – when the children are born to expat parents and travel to another country every two or three years! Mark and I, two years apart, nevertheless varied hugely in the number of schools each attended between the ages of three and eighteen (my personal and idiosyncratic indicator of stability in childhood); Mark attended five in all, and I attended ten.

Our sister, Reni, is nine years younger than me. The same doctors who experimented with my rhesus condition advised my parents about their future prospects:

'If you wait a decade before having more children, it will be like having a first child. Every cell in Mrs Landor's body will have been replaced and she will no longer produce the lethal antibodies.'

They were wrong about that too, and Reni spent the first six weeks of her life in hospital with rhesus complications.

The Mount, Ashbourne 1963; Mark, author with new sister Reni

With that age gap, it is of course to be expected that Reni had a different childhood from Mark and me; while she was growing up it must have been like having four parents instead of two siblings. Mark and I doted on her and vied with each other to entertain and care for her. Her infancy was a happy spell of childhood for all of us. In our school holidays, our mother brought afternoon tea on a rattling trolley to the sitting room, where we laid out complicated circuits for Mark's Hornby OO train set. We wound the track through the legs of Eva's grand piano, which she had given us when she moved from the family flat in Goldhurst Terrace to her smaller flat above Archway. We built towns and towers from Reni's wooden blocks, and enjoyed 'Watch with Mother' with her every lunchtime on our black-and-white TV.

The Mount garden, Ashbourne 1963; Reni, author, our dog

Mark had gone from Ghana International School to Bootham, a Quaker boarding school in York, at the age of ten. I hero-worshipped his cool friends when we visited him; one taught me how to make a tremulous owl hoot sound by blowing across my cupped hands.

When Reni's school career began, she accompanied our parents throughout her primary school years, and attended seven schools in all. In her view, this was an acceptable cost of being allowed to stay at home with our parents until she was eleven. Some expat children were sent to boarding school at eight, or even as young as four. From this time on Mark and I were with her in only one or at best two school holidays per year; we missed her dreadfully, but we followed her progress as best we could. She brought home a whole-class batch of valentines from kindergarten in New York, and a circle game she had learnt from kindergarten in Georgetown:

Rye lily waters, climbing up so high,
We all young ladies, we all must die.
Except young [name],
For she is the fairest flower of them all.

I searched junk shops and posted her the same Orlando and Babar books that I had been brought up on. The illustrations stay in my memory more strongly than the stories.

Then it was Reni's turn to be sent to boarding school. This happened the year I was living in London with my husband-to-be, J, attending Whitelands College for my Postgraduate Certificate of Education year. For want of any better inspiration, I had decided to become a teacher. I also reconnected with my Aunt Eva; I was beginning to feel like an adult, able to reach out to the women in my family and to help where I could.

One weekend I bought a day return to the station nearest to Reni's boarding school and took my little sister to tea in a local hotel. Then I took her back to school, and she showed me round. The bedrooms in her House were much less austere than the dormitories had been at my boarding school; they had individual cubicles the girls could decorate as they liked. Nevertheless, I found the visit was quite triggering. Memories of being taunted and lonely flooded back. That was still the stage where a chance sighting of a former classmate would send me fleeing into the nearest shop, heart racing and adrenaline flooding. I assumed that my past feelings of trauma were what she too was experiencing, my little sister whom I should be protecting. I felt guilty as I returned to London.

I was looking forward to telling J about my traumatic day revisiting boarding school, as I returned to the Battersea flat we shared with four others. I thought he would understand, having been one of a family of four whose childhoods had similarly been disrupted by different postings abroad; for him and his elder brother Andrew, this included boarding at first prep school then secondary school in England, when he was ten. But all thoughts of my day vanished as I found J nursing bruised fingers, black and puffy on both hands.

'That looks dreadful! What happened?'

'The sash cord in our bedroom window broke as I was opening it. It trapped both my hands between the top and bottom casements, and they were far too heavy to move. I yelled and yelled, until eventually a woman in those flats opposite us came and organised my rescue.'

Years later when we lived in Edinburgh, we met this woman again by chance. It transpired she was the journalist sister of a friend; she was visiting when we called by one evening. She and J didn't recognise each other at first, but eventually realised their connection in the trapped-finger incident through each remembering a pink Cadillac which was always parked around the corner from the flats.

This is one of those unlikely coincidences illustrating 'six degrees of separation', whereby the chain of friends of friends can supposedly connect us with any stranger in only six steps.

I am discovering the same phenomenon as I unpick the strands of what happened in my father's family some nine decades previously. Strangers are stepping forward to show me connections I had known nothing about, but that I am finding immensely comforting. Six degrees of separation are turning into networks of interlinked relationships, joining us together and showing me my roots.

On reflection, I am now coming to understand that Reni wasn't reliving my childhood; she had her own unique experience, as too did our brother. A similar realisation comes as the climax in Libby Purves' novel, *Home Leave*, set in a diplomatic family who had different postings abroad during their childhood. Trying to find a missing brother, the siblings must unpack what might have constituted his place of security, decades earlier, as it would have been different for each of them.

Eva, Stefan and Robert had different degrees of awareness in their *Elisabethstrasse* home. The Landauers had moved to this address in 1925, a few months after the birth of their second child, Stefan. So Eva, born on Boxing Day in 1922, was three when they moved there. She probably had no memories of where they had lived before this. For Stefan and Robert, this gracious apartment, where nursemaid Anny helped their mother look after them, was the only place they knew as home. Then in 1933, everything changed '...due to the massive brutality of the Nazi activists', as Dr Schier wrote. They moved first to another address in Munich, and then a few months later, to the apartment above their grandparents' department store in Landshut, *Kaufhaus Tietz*. The loss of their home was the same for each of them, but because of their ages and stages of development, the significance of this traumatic change would resonate to differing degrees through the years which followed.

In 1954, twelve years after Edith's premature death, Richard returned alone to Feldafing, that charming lakeside town in Bavaria where he and Edith had been married thirty-two years earlier. He was able to buy a property with his compensation payment from the German government. According to Dr Schier's monograph, he lived quietly, visited only by a few publisher colleagues. He corresponded with Munich poet and novelist Gottfried Kölwel about an offer from a Mr Hertz to become active again, this time as a writer rather than a publisher:

> In a sleepless night I pondered Mr Hertz' suggestion. Despite the appealing company, I don't believe I will

decide in favour of it. I am too old to start something new, particularly when it is related to language.

By then, Richard was quite deaf. The psychological and social impacts of deafness are life-changing, a massive stumbling stone to well-being; it takes a conscious effort to maintain relationships, both close and distant, when communication is disrupted in this way. Loneliness, depression, anxiety, insomnia and cognitive decline may all follow. Unless effective aids correct hearing, one result can be a loss of facility for language over time, as Richard was finding.

Deafness is a thread running through my family. My great-grandfather, Adolf Hirsch, was deaf, and according to Robert's cousin Lilli Palmer, he assuaged his resultant loneliness by bedding shop girls. My maternal grandfather Fred, shy by nature and also deaf, retreated into his solitary gardening. My mother had become deaf following the severe bout of labyrinthitis she had suffered while Mark and I were at boarding school. This was the reason she became an artist in retirement, she told me, rather than a writer; she no longer felt confident to find words she had once so enjoyed playing with, writing children's stories, songs for whiling away long car journeys, and letters for family and friends.

I too am deaf. I didn't know I was deaf, until one evening when we were visiting my parents in Ashbourne to introduce our second baby, J said,

'Listen to that owl! It must be really close.'

I could hear nothing. He raised the sash window and then – a miracle – I could hear an owl. It was such clear evidence that others could hear things that I just couldn't. I went for a hearing test, and it was confirmed. ('Completely buggered' were the actual words used by the health visitor to communicate the results, which made us both laugh. In fact, 'moderate hearing loss' is the more conventional diagnosis.) I have used hearing aids since I was thirty years old. For many years, I tried to keep them hidden, through shame and embarrassment. To me, they looked hideous, and I thought others would judge me negatively, so I always wore my hair long over my ears. It was only when I went away to Dundee University to study educational psychology, more than twenty years after my initial diagnosis, that I introduced myself to my new classmates as being deaf. The Access to Work organisation had granted me hearing equipment to help with lectures on the condition, the dispenser said, that I told any newly met people that I was deaf. It felt like a huge barrier – how would they perceive me? At fifty-one, I was already the oldest student in the cohort.

I discovered how wrong I had been all these years. On our first day, we were asked to introduce ourselves around the group. After giving a few facts about myself, I said,

'And I'm supposed to tell you, I'm deaf. I've never said this before, but I've got some fancy hearing aids and listening equipment through Access to Work, and that was their condition. These new aids are excellent, but they're not the same as natural hearing, so if I ignore something you say, it's not out of rudeness.'

One young man who had already spoken put up his hand and asked that the introductions progressing round the circle return to him. He then told us that he was completely deaf in one ear, and that hearing aids were no help; he could not hear someone speaking on his deaf side. He said he too had never told anyone before but had been inspired by my example. As we filed out of the room, another student told me I had cut her dead earlier, but now instead of being offended, she understood that I hadn't realised she was speaking.

I have noticed no particular decline in my language skills, unlike my mother. Richard's lack of confidence with language must have been a blow for one who had built his whole life around sharing words; did he understand that it may have been because of his deafness rather than his being 'too old'? If he had lived for longer, these are conversations we might have had. However, as Faulkner said in *Requiem for a Nun*, the past is never dead – it isn't even past. Even though my grandfather Richard died over sixty years ago, what I am finding out about his life and personality is developing a connection between us, a relationship.

Memories are so strange, though. I could remember the green-tiled stove in Richard's house in Feldafing because it tapped into many sensory and emotional channels. There was the physical sensation of warmth against my back after coming in from a cold damp garden. I remember the frustration of the snails escaping, and the comfort of feeling safely tucked away instead of having to sit at the dinner table with unfamiliar adults, exposed and shy. At the first meal together, my father had noticed my fear of this strange man who was trying so hard to engage me in conversation, and instead of cajoling or exhorting me to speak to my grandfather, invented a game: every time my grandfather took butter with his serrated knife, my father made a show of disapproval and smoothed it out with a straight-edged knife. Soon we were all laughing at this mock battle and the atmosphere lightened.

I could remember, too, the song our mother had invented to console me on the long journey to see *Neuschwanstein*, the fairy-tale castle of King Ludwig II of Bavaria, after I'd lost my precious balloon to the waters of Lake Feldafing:

All the balloons of Feldafing went to the lake for a swim.

All the balloons of Feldafing took off their clothes and jumped in.

They swam over to the other side.

They went to the station and caught a train and went for a ride.

Each memory is clearly preserved in my mind, and I can understand why they feel important. But why should I remember the road bending to go through an underpass? Nothing of moment happened there, and in general I am poor at remembering routes.

Psychologists continue to study the nature of memory. They now think that the human brain encodes slivers of information, which at the time of recall are then stitched into a narrative. Every time the event is summoned from memory, it is modified or added to. The present context of the person remembering, any information newly available to them, their current emotional state – these will all affect how they assemble these 'shards of coloured light' to make a picture, a story, as Fernyhough describes in his book *Pieces of Light*. Often, as I am writing, I text my older brother to ask him to clarify a memory I am struggling to grasp hold of. His honest reply is sometimes,

'But I had no idea about that until you told me about it a few years ago ... '

Thus is family history assembled from fragments that cycle around its members, gaining layers of embellishment and plausibility as the years roll by. My self-ordained task of recording the Landauer story with any veracity depends largely on the assistance of outsiders.

14

LANDSHUT, JUNE 2014

The simple invitation to visit my great-grandparents' *Stolpersteine* in Landshut triggers great excitement in our extended family. Husband, children plus a partner, a sibling and cousins all decide to come too. The size of our party – nine – prompts the Landshut city council to arrange a civic reception for us in their ancient ceremonial *Rathaus* (town hall). Our large family party arrives in small groups, travelling variously by train, plane, bus or car.

J and our son Eric and I drive there together.

'Oh god we should have turned there!'

Lorries thunder past down the *Autobahn* as the three of us peer at the fleeing road signs. The satnav is no help. A whole new motorway system must have been built since it was last updated, and now we have missed the turnoff to Landshut. We are late! Late for our own civic ceremony. Eric looks up from the map on his phone and leans between us from the back seat, trying to make sense of where we have got to.

'I think we should be ok, this way ... '

His voice tapers off. Beads of sweat spring out on my face and I see J's knuckles whiten on the steering wheel. It is in all our minds that the worst insult you can offer a German, apparently, is to be unpunctual. The city's dignitaries are gathering in their medieval *Rathaus*, waiting to bestow upon us the citizens' respect that their forebears withdrew from our family in the 1930s. We can only hope that forgiveness and reconciliation will flow in both directions.

As the family representative, I feel deeply ashamed that my group have arrived late. If only we had set off an hour earlier! We could have used any spare time to explore Landshut. I wonder now whether a deeply subconscious anxiety about this event, triggered by Hans' warning, had kept me perfecting my preparations instead of just setting off – is my hair ok? My dress? Would I fall short of what was required of me? It didn't occur to me that our hosts might be feeling a similar anxiety as to how we might view them. I rush into the *Rathaus*, blushing and stressed, to find our German hosts circling their magnificent hall, wondering – in my imagination – how to deal with this act of discourtesy.

Konrad, the chairperson of Landshut's *Stolpersteine* association who had instigated this ceremony, greets us with evident relief. He introduces us to the group of presiding officials. All can now be seated and, despite our shameful behaviour, they give us kind reassurances and the honour of the front row. Behind us sit rows of strangers, gathered together to witness this act of reparation.

At last, I can look around me. The *Prunksaal*, the main chamber of this medieval building, is decorated with murals depicting the 1475 wedding pageant of the Polish princess Jadwiga Jagiellon and Duke George of Bavaria. Plumed horses and jewelled carriages intersperse the nobles and courtiers in their richly coloured brocades. This event is re-enacted in the city every four years, in a vast pageant. Punctuating the walls of the *Rathaus*, ornate tiled stoves are set at regular intervals.

Sigi Hagl, Green Party city councillor, addresses us warmly:

'On behalf of Landshut City Council, we would like to offer a sincere welcome to you, Frau Miriam Landor, and to all your family. You are the descendants of the Hirsch and Landauer families, who were prominent citizens of Landshut and Munich.'

Next, Dr Mario Tamme, the city archivist, gives us details of the history of the two family branches – again in faultless English. (How discourteous we must seem to others in our monoglottal imperialism, I reflect, ramping up my feelings of shame.) Both speakers dwell on the importance of our visit for bringing people together and for helping us all to understand the past.

Dr Tamme gives us copies of his book *Ich bin so traurig' – Das Schicksel der Jüdischen Landshuter 1933–1942* (I am so sad – the fate of the Landshut Jewish people 1933 –1942). On the front cover are several monochrome photos, taken from identity documents. The faces are strong and beautiful, and I can recognise my great-grandmother, Cilly, and grandmother, Edith, among them.

I discover when I peruse it later that the book tells the stories of fourteen Jewish families in Landshut, devoting a chapter to each, and writing about what happened to them with devastating honesty:

> In the year 1991 one of Stefan Landauer's school friends, Anton Mößmer, wrote an essay about his school time during the Third Reich: Stefan was shunned by his classmates who were members of the *Hitler Jugend* (Hitler Youth) because as a Jew he wasn't allowed to join this association. They insulted the Jew – as they were being taught to – although they later said that they were talking about Jews in general and weren't thinking about Stefan.

Even before this sensitive young boy, my uncle, was forced to flee his home and everything he knew, he was already being bullied. Perhaps this explains his reluctance to talk about his past, I thought.

The chapter continues:

> Eva Maria went to the Ursuline middle school. As it was a convent school, she was never disadvantaged by the nuns. Erika Stadler was her best friend. The NSDAP tried to terminate this friendship by summoning Erika's father, Karl,

to the mayor. Karl refused, saying that it was impossible to prohibit contact while they were in the same school.

Karl Stadler's motivation isn't clear in this account. Was he hoping to have Eva removed from his daughter's school, by passing the responsibility back to the authorities? Or was he protecting Erika's friendship with Eva, insofar as he was able? I can only ponder, and guess. They are all long gone.

After the formal speeches are concluded, several people from the audience come forward to speak to me. One is the Green Party MP of the *Deutscher Bundestag* (the lower house of Parliament in Germany), Thomas Gambke MdB, who expresses a desire to stay in contact with me. As the Landor representative, I feel quite overwhelmed by the status and attention of the dignitaries at our civic reception, and frankly a little bewildered. I haven't yet had time to reflect on what our visit might mean to the citizens of Landshut, who are working so hard to face up to their past.

A second gift from Dr Tamme, the archivist, is a large brown paper package. Inside, I find a series of card-mounted photographs, copied from the archives. Here is a treasure trove, indeed; it is a record of every stage of the construction of my great-grandparents' house, Villa Hirsch.

It is not possible to take in the contents of the photographs during the ceremony, but I pore over them later. In all, there are seven boards of A3 size, each one showing two monochrome photographs. These are evidently copied from a photo album, as in the first one I can see a soft, tasselled string holding the plates of photos together. The frontispiece gives the name of the photographer, Josef Gottner, handwritten in white ink on the black page. Then comes the title,

Landhaus Neubau Hirsch in Bildern (Construction of the Hirsch country house in pictures), and the date, January 1929.

Landhaus Neubau Hirsch in Bildern (Hirsch new country house in pictures)

The first three photos, dated 22 June 1928, show the building site as the construction of Villa Hirsch begins. In the first, fourteen men in shirts and trousers are digging a deep hole with spades, placing soil into small carriages and smoothing over the surface ground. Most are wearing hats or caps, and a few have waistcoats. It is titled *Aushub der Baugrube* (excavation for the foundations). By coincidence, June is the same month as our visit to Landshut over eighty years later, when the weather is very pleasant: warm but not too hot.

High poles mark the corners of the planned building, and as the photographic record progresses, the hole becomes a network of trenches, boarded off for setting the concrete foundations. In the photo taken a week later, boardings of planks show where the walls are being raised, diagonal poles prop the boardings in position, and several men are working on setting more planks.

Aushub der Baugrube (Digging the foundation ditches) 22.VI.28

By 4 July, the cellar's cavity brick walls can be seen, and men are laying wooden floors on top of these walls. Trestles, barrows and wooden ramps give the builders access to the construction. A fortnight later, the shape of the large two-storey building is complete, with the brickwork finished and scaffolding supporting the men at work on the roof beams. They have not yet set doors and windows into place. This photo is taken at an angle, looking at the front left corner of the house; the long frontage is telescoped on the left of the photo and the side wall is viewed almost full on. The next photo comes from a few days later, on 3 August, and shows the back of the house still clad in scaffolding. The roof is now tiled. This is the side of Villa Hirsch that overlooks the town nestled in the valley below and faces the castle on the opposite hill, I discover later. There is a summer-room extension at the far end of the back of the building, with French doors giving access to the grounds.

The final five photos are taken four months later, in early December. They show the completed Villa Hirsch, with grey rendered walls, a glassed-in porch at the front door and plantings of walks, trees and hedges being laid out in the grounds. The attic has three small dormer windows at the front of the house, and three more at the back. I imagine these may have been servants' quarters but they have the best view! Some of the trees are mature and must have been growing there already. In a few photos, I can glimpse neighbouring villas in the distance.

The architectural style of the house is interesting. To a modern eye, it looks a little austere and barracks-like, with its symmetrical rows of small windows. I think it owes something to the *Bauhaus* philosophy of architecture, then at its height, with its plain, unadorned exterior and regular, rectangular shapes.

Villa Hirsch front view 8.XII.28

Villa Hirsch rear view 8.XII.28

We want to see Villa Hirsch for ourselves; a visit to *Brühfeldweg* in Landshut's *Annaberg* (Anna Mountain) will have to be made.

I think about my great-grandmother, Cilly, living in Villa Hirsch and managing its day-to-day organisation. Folded among the pack of letters, rosettes and random scraps I had been given was a handmade, collaged card. The base is a printed image of a stylised Viking prow, its white head rearing high against a bright, cerulean blue background of sky and sea. Birds wheel overhead. Cilly had cut out figures from black-and-white photos and glued them into position, looking out from the deck. There stand my father's family, Richard, Edith, Eva, Stefan and Robert, the children each wearing a scarf and a woolly hat. Under the picture, Cilly wrote these words:

Möge unsere geliebte Tochter, ihr Schiff
unter Leitung der Friedenstaube mit Mann
u. Kindern immer den sicheren Hafen gesund
erreichen!

(May our beloved daughter, / her ship under the guidance of the dove of peace, / with husband and children, / ever securely reach safe harbour!)

Cilly's farewell card

Grandfather Richard is staring straight at the photographer, whilst my grandmother, Edith, is looking towards the horizon, where her future awaits. Eva stands between her two brothers. All three children are smiling as they look back down the length of the ship, perhaps relieved to be leaving behind them the nightmare that life in their homeland had become. The children look as if they are enjoying this adventure, but the adults must have asked themselves whether this parting from their loved ones would be final – as indeed it was.

I can imagine my father, then aged eleven, asking why his *Opa* and *Oma* (grandfather and grandmother) were not with them; the Landauer and Hirsch families would have become very close in the five years they had lived in Landshut. Would he have understood why his grandparents were staying behind? What could be more important than escaping to freedom from the persecution that now threatened their daily lives? He had been allowed to keep his plush toy monkey, the violin that he was learning to play and his paperweight containing Toby the lizard, embalmed for ever in a heavy glass capsule. These had been packed up with all their most precious family possessions: the monogrammed linen from his mother's trousseau; a few portraits and family photographs; the mantelpiece clock; the best Rosenthal china, and silver cutlery. His father's copies of *Delphin-Verlag* art books took up much of the space.

It must have been so puzzling for Robert. Five years previously, they had left Munich to live above the department store belonging to his grandparents in Landshut. In *Elisabethstrasse*, the ceilings were high, the rooms were spacious and their nursemaid, Anny, lived with them to look after them. His grandparents' house, Villa Hirsch, overlooking Landshut from the hill above, was also huge and gracious. It had wonderful gardens to play and hide in, but their apartment above the department store was small and poky. The Landauers were, of course, more fortunate than so many, but Robert was too young to appreciate that. However, even at eleven he must have understood on some level why they had to leave Germany: because the Nazis had stopped Jews like them from earning their living and had imprisoned or attacked them. Jewish people, old and young, rich and poor, were being forced to stitch a yellow Star of David to their clothing, to add the names 'Sarah' or 'Israel' on their official papers. But he probably didn't feel Jewish – his family was Christian, fully assimilated into German society, and they had never followed Jewish religious observance. Robert's sister Eva went to a Catholic convent school when they lived in Landshut, and he and his big brother, Stefan, attended the Jesuit Hans Carossa school.

Perhaps he wondered what their destination in Parsifal Road, London, would be like. His grandmother's sister's family already lived there, following their flight from Berlin – Great-Aunt Rose and her three daughters, Irene, Lilli and Hilde. Would there be room for the five Landauers too? As I bring my thoughts back from the imaginings of the past that Cilly's card for Edith has prompted, other pictures come to mind. Perhaps we are becoming numb to the sight of a grieving parent cradling the body of a drowned child; numb to the images of frail overcrowded barques of humanity, carrying people no different from ourselves who are attempting to gain freedom at the risk of life. I look again at Cilly's brave goodbye card to her daughter, as the little family prepares to cross an ocean to an enemy's land; I see today's refugees, still fleeing with whatever few possessions they can salvage from their former lives. It is impossible to understand how this can still be happening throughout the world, century after century.

15

VISIT TO STUMBLING STONES AND SCHOOL; LANDSHUT, JUNE 2014

There remains one last part of our formal civic reception. Young women bearing baskets of flowers hand each of us a posy. Audience, officials and Landors, we all walk from the *Rathaus* in *Aldstadt* across the wide street to the former *Kaufhaus Tietz* department store in *Theaterstrasse*. We have seen photos of the department store as it was when newly constructed by my great-grandfather; it had ornate turrets and crenelations, reminding me somewhat of Jenners in Edinburgh's Princes Street. By now, the edifice had been rebuilt in a plain 'Art Deco' style to fit in with the surrounding shops, giving a harmonious street of coloured shopfronts. And there, set into the pavement in front of the plate-glass window, are two *Stolpersteine*, engraved brass plaques each the size of a cobble stone. These are the first 'stumbling stones' I have ever seen, and I bend over to read the inscribed text:

HIER ARBEITETE ADOLF HIRSCH JG. 1868
DEPORTIERT 1942 THERESIENSTADT TOT 22.9.1943

HIER ARBEITETE CÄCILIE HIRSCH GEB. LISSMAN
JG. 1876 GEDEMÜTIGT / ENTRECHTET FLUCHT
IN DEN TOD 30.10.1941

I translated these words in my mind as:
Here worked Adolf Hirsch, born 1868, deported 1942 Theresienstadt, dead 22.9.1943.

Here worked Cäcilie Hirsch *née* Lissman, born 1876, humiliated / disenfranchised fled into death 30.10.1941'.

Adolf and Cäcilie (Cilly) Hirsch Stolpersteine

It is difficult to get my face right – to play the part of a grateful guest at a reception in my honour, while taking in the full tragedy described in these words. Should I carry on smiling? I can feel it becoming rictus-like before it fades. I wish I were alone, so I could understand what I'm reading. My elderly great-grandfather had been deported to the infamous ghetto Theresienstadt, a transit station on the way to the extermination camps, where he had died. My great-grandmother Cilly had been humiliated, disenfranchised, and had fled into death. What did that mean? Had she been chased by someone and died whilst fleeing? Or had she died by suicide? These are indeed 'stumbling stones' to my peace of mind, and I need to find out more.

We have little time to reflect as the next part of the programme is go for lunch with the vice-chairperson, teacher Franz Gervasoni, and some of his final year history students. They have also attended the ceremony in the *Rathaus*. Franz has booked a long table in a restaurant's shady courtyard, and we arrange ourselves so the younger members of our family party sit among the school students. Franz watches them with a benign expression, as his protégés practise their English and their social skills.

Then he leans forward and whispers to me:

'I am so pleased that they came to this morning's ceremony and now to lunch. Today is actually a school holiday, so they are giving up their day off. This is the second group who have selected the Jews of Landshut as their final history project; it was another group of my history students who requested *Stolpersteine* for remembrance. This group made an exhibition 'A Part of Us' about the fates of the Jewish people here in Landshut. You see, they felt they really wanted to do something, in the light of what they were learning about their hometown, their relatives, their neighbours. It was not a simple task. A descendant of Nazi sympathisers, now in a powerful position in our town, objected to his forebears being named, and much diplomacy and strength of will was required.'

I would like to ask for more details, but he moves smoothly on, and I lose the opportunity.

'They will accompany us to our school afterwards, if you would like to see the school records we found for Stefan and Robert?'

I feel very touched by the actions of these young people. They have demonstrated an evident desire to right a wrong done by the townspeople of their great-grandparents' generation; to do this through their school studies seems exceptional. The students could have concentrated on turning in a good-enough project for their final marks, but instead they had written letters, raised funds and organised an association 'Against Forgetting'. They had researched and created a public exhibition, encountering negative attitudes towards their attempts at 'truth and reconciliation' from people in power in their own community, but with the support of their teachers, they had withstood them.

I am beginning to realise how wrong I was in thinking that the war was finished and done with long ago; for the present generation of Germans, it still carries wounds that need to be lanced and salved. Adolescence, in particular, is a time when idealistic passions are at their height, along with a desire to create a better world than the one they are discovering. What must these teenagers have felt as they discovered what their current wellbeing and prosperity had been built on? That properties and possessions had been taken from ordinary people – those who they recognised had been 'a part of us' – to be expropriated by their own kinsfolk and neighbours? In addition, the students are continuing to see it through by being with us on our day of civic honour, despite it being a school holiday, and by welcoming us to their city. What great ambassadors they are for a new Europe, where nations should live in peace with each other and protect all marginalised peoples! It feels especially relevant to reflect on the 1930s march of fascism, because current conditions in many countries seem to match those danger signals ignored by my great-grandparents' generation. A widening differential of prosperity between those in power and those living in vulnerable conditions is again leading to the 'othering' of people from different races and religions, invoking populist fears of stolen jobs and homes. Are we sleepwalking into conflict again, I wonder? I look round the table at the bright young faces and hope these burgeoning friendships will make a difference.

We readily accept Franz' invitation to visit their school, and we all make our way there after the pleasant lunch has drawn to a close. The Jesuits founded the Hans-Carossa Gymnasium in 1629. It is now a flourishing high school, specialising in linguistic, humanistic and science & technology studies. I note that all three Landauer children went to Catholic schools, and were fully assimilated with all the other Bavarian children of that time.

Franz leads our family party and his students to a comfortable staff room, empty because of the school holiday, and we settle ourselves to listen to his presentation. He tells us a little of the school's prestigious history, and of some famous – and infamous – alumni:

'Heinrich Himmler, who was born in 1900, was a pupil here. His father was the deputy principal of this school.'

In Wikipedia it says that 'Other boys at the school later remembered him as studious, and awkward in social situations.' The young Adolf Hitler had also felt rejected, I remember, in his case by the art world. Might genuine social inclusion prevent sociopathic behaviour from developing, I wonder? Then we are shown some of the display boards produced by the students for their 'A Part of Us' exhibition. Stefan, shunned by his classmates, had not been accepted as a part of them; he had not turned into a monster like Himmler, but neither had he been able to forgive the country of his birth.

Franz produces copies of school records for the two brothers, Stefan and Robert. To my surprise, my father was a higher achiever than his older brother in those school years. Whereas Stefan had gone on to a prestigious career as a chemistry professor specialising in amines and amino acids, my father was quite a slow reader and writer. He was a doer rather than an academic. Through my work as an educational psychologist, I know that experiencing trauma has a major impact on learning. If a child is being hurt, emotionally or physically, if they are distressed or on high alert for danger, their brains are 'unavailable for learning' and they cannot pay attention or process information. During those years at the Hans-Carossa-Gymnasium, we have Anton Mößmer's admission that Stefan was being bullied, which must have had an impact on his studies. No wonder he performed less well than his happier little brother.

My father attended the Hans-Carossa School until he was ten, and evidently did well there. I can't help comparing it to my own early years, dotting between England, Kenya and Ghana. After Robert's tour of volunteering in Kenya, he returned home briefly to collect us; he had secured a paid post in Kenya and this time we could join him. I was three years old. Journeys to and from Kenya were made by ocean liner, travelling through the Suez Canal, in the days before air travel became affordable for ordinary people. The voyage to Mombasa, on an Italian ship, gave rise to my very first conscious memory, of towering bunk beds in our family's cabin. I remember, too, the friendly Italian waiters insisting that even small children should try pasta and watered-down red wine, both new experiences for this family from 1950s Cheshire.

My young parents were hungry for adventure, and every weekend took us out exploring the bush, the countryside of Kenya. We visited the Game Park and the Leakeys' palaeontological dig, the Serengeti Plain and the Ngorongoro Crater, sometimes travelling as a family and sometimes with various international friends. On one trip, we were encamped with another family in the Rift Valley; we children were being bathed in a tin tub in the sleeping-hut, when a huge trumpeting and squealing filled the air.

'I do wish the men would stop teasing the elephants,' the other woman said, panic evident in her heightened voice.

'Shh,' said my mother. 'It's quite alright.'

Even though I was only four, I could tell she was trying to reassure us children but was pretty scared herself.

Our father took great pride in our car, a huge ancient Jaguar that gulped down petrol but had a silver statue of a pouncing jaguar soaring from its black bonnet. One evening Robert slowed down to allow a herd of giraffe to cross the road in front of us, but as he gathered speed again, a straggling baby giraffe galloped up. It straddled the bonnet as it tried and failed to leap over the car, then hobbled away into the bush. It was surely lion-prey soon after. We spent the rest of the journey picking slivers of windscreen glass out of our legs as we mourned the baby's fate.

Quakerism was still important in our parents' lives, even with all the adventures to be enjoyed. We often attended Friends meetings on Sunday, in an open-sided, grass-thatched Meeting Room, welcoming the breeze as it rustled through surrounding trees.

By the time we left in 1959, some aspects of life were improving for Kenyans, although their old ways, which had served well until the white man's coming, had been irrevocably eroded; assimilation was taking place. In the June newsletter of the Friends Service Council, it was reported that:

Former Mau Mau detainees living in the new rice growing villages of the Mwea Plain may now expect a cash crop return of £160 a year per family from a four-acre plot instead of the equivalent of £40 a year from the original subsistence farming on the then undeveloped land. In the swimming pools of Nairobi, black, brown and white bodies disport in the same water and, in the cafés of the Government Road, people of all races chat and argue over coffee and cakes. The first two African and Asian girls to be admitted into the European Girls' High School at Limuru are reported to be enjoying themselves there.

And in many ways, there has been an easing of tensions which would have seemed unimaginable in 1954 when British Friends first began work in Kenya ...

The hostels for the [Royal East African Technical] College, to the building of which the Asian communities have subscribed half a million as a memorial to Mahatma Gandhi, are to be run on multiracial lines. The only other example of this sort in education is the little Preparatory School for boys and girls at Hospital Hill, started by a German attender at the Nairobi Friends Meeting and helped by Margaret Porter and others. Surely there ought not to be the segregation that persists among Kenyan boys and girls?

I realise now that my parents were making a statement in enrolling Mark at Hospital Hill School. He was escorted every day by our 'houseboy' (what an insulting term for an adult!) who carried the statutory large lunch Thermos, with its three internal aluminium pots containing each course. There are photos of Mark in a white shirt, grey shorts and blue tie, waving a Union Jack for the visit of the young Princess Margaret in 1956.

When I was old enough, I went to Hospital Hill School too, for a brief spell before we left Kenya – my third school before I was six years old. My first nursery teacher, Mrs Epsom, who had taught me to read and to do simple arithmetic, had suggested that my parents move me to another nursery school. She said she couldn't help making a favourite of me, her very first pupil. She went on to teach Jomo Kenyatta's family. I hated my second nursery school, perhaps unsurprisingly if I was no longer treated as special. I remember they made us stay outside at break time, where the grassy bank we sat on had biting ants. The move from this second nursery school to Hospital Hill School came as a relief.

Small children don't notice lofty idealism or skin colour, and they accept their companions without thinking. As an adult, though, I am aware that even in this integrated environment we were still part of a privileged elite.

There followed the six months in London when we lived with Eva, in the family flat in Goldhurst Terrace, Swiss Cottage, before my father got another post abroad. This second tour of expat service took our family to Ghana, on the west coast. Ghana had gained its independence in 1957, the first African country to do so. Robert secured a contract in 1959 to work for the British government's Department for Overseas Development, helping set up social services in Ghana, and training and supporting Africans to run their own organisations. My father later explained to me that he and Margaret were far happier there than they had been in Kenya, as the community they now moved in was more mixed. Many of their new friends were African. Kenyan society had been less integrated, despite the efforts of some. My brother, Mark, and I attended Ghana International School, and standing in line every day under the fierce sun and the Ghanaian flag, learnt to sing the national anthem of that time:

Lift high the flag of Ghana,
The gay star shining in the sky,
Bright with the souls of our fathers,
Beneath whose shade we'll live and die.
Red for the blood of the heroes in the fight,
Green for the fruitful farms of our birthright,
And linked with these the shining golden band
That marks the richness of our Fatherland.

I loved the bright colours of the Ghanaian flag, the red, yellow and green stripes with the black star in the centre, although when I listen to it now on YouTube, the tune sounds rather western. At home, we preferred highlife, with its local instruments and voices and syncopated rhythms. Highlife is a fusion of Ghanaian ethnic folk and tribal music, and the jazz and blues music imported after the Second World War. African drums, *seperewa*, the harp-lute, and *gankogul*, the bell, are combined with guitars and jazz wind instruments. In those immediate post-independence years, the Ghanaian government promoted highlife as a tool for forging a national identity. My favourite LP of that time, from when I was six years old, was by the Tropical Rhythm Blackbeats Band. The album sleeve shows a typical Ghanaian scene, of African children playing on an expanse of golden sand, under soaring coconut palms. It reminds me of Labadi, Accra's town beach, where every week my mother used to take a group of Ghanaian children who otherwise had no access to play, jam-packed into her tiny Fiat car.

Ghanaian highlife LP

Before that, when we lived in Kenya, we had also listened to African music – an LP called Something New from Africa, featuring Little Lemmy Special on his penny whistle. So, from the 78 rpm discs of classical Bach choir music and the baroque music of Vivaldi that had brought my parents together, they adventured to new modes and beats. They shared their discoveries with us children on newly minted 33 1/3 rpm long-playing records.

During our time in Ghana, my parents must have realised that their adventurous expat lifestyle had its disadvantages as well. They bought a dilapidated villa in Ashbourne, on a hill overlooking the town (like Villa Hirsch), and began renovating it. Fred and Mabel, my grandparents, built themselves a bungalow in the walled garden at the bottom of the large grounds. For brief spells during home leave, I attended the local independent PNEU school, just around the corner from our house. Perhaps they wanted to give their children a taste of the stability my mother had grown up with, instead of mirroring the insecurity experienced by Stefan and Robert during their time at Hans-Carossa school.

16

VILLA HIRSCH; LANDSHUT, JUNE 2014

The planned programme draws to a close, and Franz asks if he and Konrad can meet with me once more before our departure. The young people exchange contact details, and we part with warm expressions of friendship. (Almost a decade later, we are still in touch with one of these students, Johanna, and she and our daughter, Naomi, regularly contact each other, exchanging presents for the next generation, their children).

As arranged, Konrad and Franz are waiting for me in the museum's courtyard the following day. Konrad has a cloth bag over his shoulder, and from it he draws an antique, fabric-covered hardback book. It is a little smaller than A4, with an elongated snowflake-like pattern stamped on its covers, brown on cream. Impressed on the centre of the front cover are capital letters in a black, Art Deco typeface, spelling out the words *ALFRED KUHN – DIE NEUERE PLASTIK* (Alfred Kuhn – New Sculpture).

'I have brought this to give to you,' Konrad says shyly. 'It is from the *Delphin-Verlag* press. Your grandfather published it. He gave us so many beautiful books...'

I can barely stammer out my thanks, feeling so touched by his thoughtful gift. This volume triggers my own precious collection of *Delphin-Verlag* books, which I gather over the next few years.

We take our leave of this kind pair, who have done so much to restore our family heritage to us, smoothing out the stumbling stones of past tragedy. It is time to explore Landshut and most importantly, to search for Villa Hirsch. We begin at Trausnitz Castle, founded in 1204 and set on a hill above Landshut. The very name *Landshut* means 'to protect the land' – *die Hut* translates as care, keeping, protection – and any intruders would have been visible from a long distance because of the castle's prominent position.

Above the valley in which the city centre nestles is another high hill, *Annaberg*, and it is there we head for next. Using the navigation tools on our phones, we wander along *Brühfeldweg*, admiring the large villas set in extensive gardens, and searching for the right one. There is no sign on the house, and we have to work out which one it is by counting on from the few houses which display a number. The one we decide must be Villa Hirsch is indeed a beautiful house, but it looks nothing like the grey, fortress-like photos of its early years. Added now are a huge, two-storey wing at right angles to the main building facing the road, two separate large garage blocks, and cream-coloured render over everything.

'I'm not sure this can be right – it looks nothing like the photos, from this side anyhow,' I say.

We look around for someone to ask but the road is empty. Perhaps we might find it easier to check it against the photos if we could see the house from the back too, I think.

'Let's just have a quick peep round the other side – that's the aspect I think I'd recognise. The front looks nothing like the original photos.'

My family stare at me, looking scandalised.

'You can't go in there – that's trespassing!'

To my delight, my cousin Francis backs me up.

'There's no one around. And we can go through the trees... Come on!'

Feeling very daring, the two of us creep around the side of the building, through a stand of pine trees. Soft needles dampen the sounds of our footfall, with just an occasional crack of a twig to jolt our hearts. We look back at the others, standing on the pavement and scanning the deserted street, and we edge forward again – and there is Cilly's summer house! This little building, with a curved lead roof, appears in the photo album my mother labelled, and also in the construction photos the archivist, Dr Tamme, gave me. Unlike the smart main building, the summer house looks rather dilapidated. My heart goes out to it. I imagine restoring it to make a studio and spending my summers there, stepping in my family's very footsteps. It is a project I intend to pursue.

Cilly's summer house 2014

Back in Switzerland, I remember having read an entertaining memoir by Lilli Palmer, the film actor, writer and artist. Lilli was related to my father; her mother, Rose Lissman, was a sister of my great-grandmother,

Cäcilie, and so Lilli was Cilly's niece, a first cousin once removed to my father. After leaving Germany for London with her mother and her two sisters, Lilli had starred in British films in the 1930s, before being taken up by Hollywood. She was married for a while to Rex Harrison, the English actor, whom I had loved seeing in the part of Professor Higgins in the film of My Fair Lady. When I was a teenager, it was Lilli's witty style of writing and her anecdotes of the rich and famous that appealed to me. Now I am more interested in the early chapters, where she describes her family and her childhood years, so I seek out a copy. *Change Lobsters and Dance* was published in 1974 in German under the title *Dicke Lilli – Gutes Kind* (Fat Lilli – Good Child). The following year the newly titled translation was brought out in America. The paperback I now buy second-hand was published in 1977 and had the strapline 'A wonderfully detached, funny book about her life before, with and after Rex Harrison'. But this time around, I focus my attention less on her famous husband and rather on a few paragraphs in chapter two, headed 'A Decent Family'.

Lilli explains that her mother, Rose, was the youngest of five sisters, and that:

> Right from the start, Cilly, the second sister, mothered them all. Even as a young girl, Cilly had a quiet authority, an outward serenity that made her look after, protect and promote any person who came her way.

In an illustrative anecdote, the five sisters, following their mother's death, travelled with her ashes from Frankfurt to Landshut, chattering all the way, to recuperate at Cilly's home, Villa Hirsch (where we had just stood). Changing trains in Munich, they left the urn on the train compartment's luggage rack, and only discovered its loss on their arrival in Landshut. They had to retrace their journey all the way to the now dark railway yard in Munich, before at last achieving their goal:

Tucked safely under Cilly's arm was Mama.

My great-grandmother was indeed the one everyone could rely on to put things right.

My parents had visited Lilli Palmer and her second husband, Carlos, at their home in Switzerland in 1970, when Robert was working at the United Nations headquarters in Geneva. Lilli had been delighted to meet more family members. I can imagine that seeing the grandson of her favourite aunt made the occasion doubly precious to her. I am beginning to feel an enormous pride in belonging to the family of Cilly and of Lilli. And it feels extraordinary to have stood in front of the family home, Villa Hirsch, with Cilly's summer house just a few metres away.

17

IMPORTANCE OF FAMILY MEMORIES; REFLECTION

Spurred on by Hans' email, which I shared with my siblings, my brother Mark explores what documents had fallen to his share after our mother's death. He comes upon the genealogical table of Moses Samuel Landauer, born in 1808, our great-great-grandfather: *Des Nachfahren des Moses Samuel Landauer und seine Ehefrau Klara aus Hürben bei Krumbach* (The descendants of Moses Samuel Landauer and his wife Klara of Hürben bei Krumbach). The ancient village of Hürben, now part of the neighbouring town, Krumbach, is in Bavarian Swabia. Until the Third Reich, it had a higher percentage of Jewish inhabitants than the rest of Bavaria. This was a place where Jewish people could feel safe, and prosper. I wonder whether my parents had chosen my name, Miriam Sharon Landor, to match the initials of our prestigious ancestor, Moses Samuel Landauer?

The Landauer family tree has full biographical annotations, tabulated as: forename, family name, maiden name; dates of birth, marriage, death; places of birth and death; profession. Only one of the seventy or so women has a profession: opera singer. The other women have a dash in that column. Of the men, around half are textile manufacturers, as was Moses Samuel himself. The others are mainly merchants, with a few bankers, traders and one cantor. I remember my mother telling me that a Landauer was the first to introduce the new jacquard weaving to Germany. This used a mechanised loom, thus doing away with the need for child labour. It seemed that many Jewish people channelled their abilities into manufacturing and trade. Here was a similarity to

Robert's adopted Quakerism. The early Friends were prevented from entering professions, and instead set up companies such as Rowntree and Cadbury, model social employers and beacons of ethical practice of their day.

Quakerism had appealed to Robert on many levels. He had a robust faith allied to a strong moral code. Robert and his brother, Stephen, had experienced name-calling and bullying in the street and at school during their London childhood. He must have felt accepted and respected in this sect, which has no liturgy or hierarchy – no longer an outcast.

Popular understanding of prejudice, such as they experienced as child refugees, comes from such psychological studies as Sherif's summer camp experiments of the 1950s. By dividing the summer camp boys into different groups and making them compete, an in-group – out-group mentality developed, with the children displaying barbaric behaviour like in William Golding's 1954 *Lord of the Flies*. Those in the in-group saw those in the out-group as different, to be shunned. Taking an example from the natural world, a healthy flock will peck and drive away a sick duckling. However, contemporary reviewers such as Rutger Bregman (*Humankind: A Hopeful History*) have analysed the original accounts of the experiments and found serious methodological flaws: camp supervisors followed instructions to stamp out any pro-social intentions among the boys, such as 'Maybe we could make friends with those guys'. I could only hope that the Landauer children, too, had been offered some hands in friendship.

Bregman's premise is that most people are decent, that a crisis brings out the best in us, that it takes particular circumstances and malevolent persuasion over a long time to corrupt humanity's basic desire to help each other. In particular, he considers the Holocaust in the light of Milgram's electric shock experiments, in which ordinary people inflicted severe pain on others when ordered to by powerful authority figures. This was thought to explain why so many German people had obeyed even the most inhumane orders of the Nazis. Bregman's review of the experimental records showed that the statement that achieved the greatest obedience was 'The experiment requires that you continue'; the direct order 'You have no other choice, you must go on' provoked instant disobedience. Subsequent interviews with participants showed that they thought they were benefiting science for the greater good of humankind when they agreed to take part in the experiment. Bregman concludes that most people are indeed capable of doing evil if manipulated or pushed hard enough, but that first it must be disguised as doing good.

Cognitive scientist Steven Pinker argues similarly that humankind has made progress overall, in terms of kindness, wellbeing and peace; we no longer burn witches and bait dancing bears, on the whole (*The Better Angels of our Nature: Why Violence has Declined*, 2010). This kind of optimism was my father's typical outlook too, and I imbibed it throughout my childhood. Now I am asking myself, but what is evil? How is it seeded and what should we do to prevent it from taking root?

It is clear from reading Robert's letters how close the relationship between these brothers was: 'I always feel that we four [Robert and Stephen and their partners]... '; 'I do feel awfully sorry for you... '; 'All my love, your Robert'. I can fully understand how shared adversity and separation from loved ones brings about a strong bond and interdependence. Until I started at boarding school myself, Mark and I were not particularly close. Indeed, as is the way of big brothers everywhere, a regular entertainment for him was to test how far my gullibility would take me.

Mark: Why don't you get some more sweeties for us from the drawer – we're allowed ...

Me: OK.

Robert: Who's been at the after-lunch treat drawer – you know you're only allowed one each and now they're all gone!

Me: But he told me to …

My father used to sigh as he scolded me for each misdemeanour instigated by my brother:

Robert: And if he told you to jump off a cliff, would you do it?

Me: No, but Daaad …

All that changed when I was twelve and sent to boarding school in my turn. We spent either one or two school holidays each year being farmed out to friends or grandparents. Trips back home to our parents in Africa or the Americas were only funded by employers once a year, when we flew halfway across the world, unaccompanied. At the beginning we experienced the humiliation of being an 'unaccompanied minor', having to wear a huge eye-catching label around our necks. But quite quickly, we were deemed competent to cope by ourselves, and off we went. We would snuggle up under the airplane blankets in the long hours of darkness, leaning on each other.

I remember one trip when, as teenagers, we stopped for a few days in New York and stayed with my father's cousin, Dora, on our way to join our family in Guyana. She had married the publisher, Ted Schocken, and they had three grown-up daughters. Dora prepared a homemade advocaat every morning for her husband as a health cure, beating an egg into sweetened brandy and vanilla. We looked on enviously, wishing our family's breakfasts were as sophisticated.

On another occasion, flying to spend the school summer vacation in Zambia, we were set down for an unscheduled day at Entebbe Airport in Uganda, later the scene of the notorious hijack. It was an empty shack at that time, and we had nothing to do except wait, huddled together sitting on our cases and looking out onto a blinding, sun-scorched runway. When at last we flew on to Nairobi, our host, my old nursery teacher, Mrs Epsom, drove us past our old house, where we had lived during our time in Kenya.

'Is that it?' we said. 'But it's tiny ... '

It was indeed very much smaller, and much more basic, than Bobbin Cottage where we had lived until I was three. It made me realise afresh how courageous, and altruistic, my parents were, as they left behind security and familiarity to help others.

There came a time when neither Mark nor I had heard from our mother for some weeks. We met up at York Minster on a Sunday *exeat* from our respective boarding schools, and swapped notes.

'When was your last letter from Mum?'

'Weeks and weeks ago.'

'Mine too ... Something must be really wrong.'

Our father was abroad, and she was on her own in Ashbourne at that time, supposedly helping her parents. Mark decided to ask for that unheard-of luxury, a phone call home. It turned out that she had indeed been very ill with severe labyrinthitis causing a total loss of balance and hearing, following a gallstone operation. But she 'hadn't wanted to worry us' so hadn't told us children, and no one else realised that we were being kept in the dark – with the result that ever afterwards the slightest delay in correspondence caused us to panic, fearing the worst. When appealed to, our father agreed that it was always better to be told what was happening, but we never succeeded in changing our mother's behaviour in such circumstances. Perhaps as an only child, she was more used to coping on her own than to reaching out for help, whereas siblings have the luxury of depending on each other.

As adolescence continued, my brother and I became each other's close friend and confidante. His being two years older was useful – he could drive me to our evening's entertainment with our friends, and we could both eye up each other's mates. When I was sixteen and at a residential sixth-form college, our parents decided we were old enough to live independently in the holidays. They arranged a flat for us in half of our family home in Ashbourne, whilst three older friends, one of whom I was dating, shared the other half. At last, life felt very good. We learnt to play bridge, went to funfairs and stock car races, and made dinners together as a fivesome.

Yet not long after that happy time, everything fell apart for me. I was about to begin university, and Mark went across the world to spend a year in Australia. Once again, major disruptions occurred in my education. In September 1971, I had missed achieving one of my required A level grades, so could not take up my offer of a place for a triple degree in maths, French and English at Sheffield University. I know now that I should have just phoned them, and asked to be given a chance, or to drop the weaker of the three subjects, but in those days, people like us never dreamt of challenging authority.

Instead, I started at North London Polytechnic College, in Red Lion Square, to study an ordinary degree in French and Arabic. They gave those of us who had no prior knowledge of Arabic a two-week total immersion course in the run-up to the official beginning of term. My digs weren't available until term started, so I spent the time in a caravan site for homeless students in south London, still empty before the normal start of term. The weather was hot, the windows wouldn't open and the green plastic curtains melted and stank, but I was too terrified to open the door. I also starved myself, as I was so shocked at London prices for food. It was my grandparents' golden wedding anniversary back home in Ashbourne, but I refused to go, not being able to handle the thought of a journey home and an immediate return to London; I was barely holding it together.

Towards the end of the introductory fortnight, things were improving. An old school friend from primary school days had offered me her floor in her student hall of residence. I was enjoying the Arabic course ('*Ana bint! Ana wallad!*' I am a girl! I am a boy!) and making friends among the widely-differing students; my buddy group included a boy from a Romany travelling family and a middle-aged wife and mother.

Then UCCA, the university clearing house, contacted my parents to offer me a last-minute place at Royal Holloway College to read a French honours degree: ' ... we're so sorry, Mrs Landor, we lost your daughter's name.' My mother accepted on my behalf, believing an honours degree would always be better than an ordinary one, so I moved to Surrey, just as my brother was leaving for his year on the other side of the world. Looking back now, I wonder what my life would have been if I'd completed the degree course I had started, achieving fluency in both French and Arabic, following six-month placements in each of Cairo and Paris. In the event, I quickly changed course from my weaker subject, French, to English language and literature, and finished with a 2:1 – surely a far less advantageous preparation for adult life.

That was yet another upheaval – a new place, new people, and three educational programmes to get to grips with, in the space of three weeks. I had never felt so alone. My periods stopped, and I feared I might be pregnant, although that would have been an impossibility from the very little physical contact I'd had on a date; I was quite ignorant in those pre-internet days. It felt so hard to have to start all over again to make friends. The song on everyone's lips that year was Carole King's You've Got a Friend. But there was no point in calling a name; my best friend, my brother, couldn't come. I had to grow up and learn how to stand on my own feet.

That period in my life gave me an understanding of how important a sibling relationship can be. Of course, in some circumstances, the sibling relationship may be toxic and damaging to one or both; decisions about how to place children when families break up are very complex. There can be no doubt about the strength of the relationship between Robert and his older brother, though. In the letter written from his summer job, cherry-picking in Kent, Robert referred to his sadness that they have found themselves on opposite sides in the split family household; he finished:

You know the spirit of love and friendship in which this letter was written.

This pair must have depended on each other through their years of shared experience and trauma, just as I had done with my brother.

18

LEAVING SWITZERLAND WITH FRESH TASKS; JULY 2014

Once we are back in Switzerland following our Landshut visit, Hans translates for me some of the literature we have been given. The principal source of information was a glossy, A4 booklet about the laying of the first *Stolpersteine* in Landshut. This event had taken place in October 2012, almost two years before our visit. It contains brief biographies of the families being thus commemorated. I turn eagerly to the pages about Cäcilie and Adolf Hirsch.

It begins with a quotation from the local newspaper, under the headline 'Well-liked and respected by the population – tracing the Landshut Jews':

> Jews living in Landshut were fully integrated and highly respected by the Landshut population, particularly because of their social engagement, and they were well-liked. Foremost, Adolf Hirsch, owner of the largest department store in Landshut, had made a name for himself as a benefactor of the town and of the poor.

The article refers to Adolf's appointment as an honorary member of the *Turngemeinde* (Sports Club). Hans explains in a footnote that such membership was regarded as a powerful statement of a patriotic German attitude, and that being appointed an honorary member was an explicit compliment.

The Hirsch couple had three children. Kurt, later a well-known pianist and conductor, was the eldest, followed by Edith, who became my grandmother. Their youngest son, Erich, died in infancy. Wealth and prestige cannot protect you from desperate tragedy and grief, I thought. (Entirely coincidentally, some forty years ago, we named our second son Eric.) Adolf owned successful shops in Gera and in Munich, and took over the department store, *Kaufhaus Tietz*, in Landshut in 1892, five years before his marriage to Cäcilie Lissman. In the following years, he acquired more land in the city centre and extended the shop premises, demolishing a residential building to do so.

The new building was magnificent. It had four storeys, a basement and an attic, with a lift connecting the main floors. The ground floor featured a glass-covered atrium, and a wide staircase of massive oak wood and oaken wall panels led from the atrium to the first floor.

Landshut a. d. Isar im Festkleid. Kaufhaus Tietz

Hermann Tietz Nachfolger, the Hirsches' department store, Landshut

Adolf's next project was to build himself a house worthy of such a prominent businessman: Villa Hirsch. I remember my father telling us of his grandparents' Great Dane, the size of a child's pony, who could open all the door handles with her mouth and thus roam around the premises:

> We were always finding her in the oddest places! She was very gentle and had a sweet nature so no one could ever be scared of her.

The Landauer photo album compiled later by my mother shows many family occasions from that time; the children got dressed up for theatrical shows in the villa, and their father, Richard, down on his hands and knees, gave them horsey rides on his back in the well-kept grounds. They looked so happy and informal in these scenes from their new life, under the protection of Grandfather Adolf, and far enough away from the growing unease of Munich.

Games in Villa Hirsch garden

As Adolf grew older, he became increasingly deaf, and in 1933 appointed his son-in-law, Richard, as one of two new co-directors of the *Kaufhaus Tietz* department store. When Richard took up this new post, it must have been a relief to have had an income again to support his family, but I'm sure he would have been in mourning for his beloved *Delphin-Verlag*. Their attic apartment above the department store was so different from their gracious *Elisabethstrasse* home in Munich.

The Nazi storm clouds were gathering over Landshut too, despite Adolf's prestigious position. Eventually Eva could not go out to meet her friend Erika Stadler. They could only communicate through messages placed at the bottom of a basket that Eva pulled up on a string to their attic apartment. When I eventually stand by the department store, looking down at the *Stolpersteine* for Eva's grandparents, I visualise the lonely teenage girl leaning from a small window high above, her only friend standing on the pavement below; they both know that this meeting could put their families in danger but nevertheless are desperate for a moment of connection.

As the prohibition on Jews owning businesses took force, *Kaufhaus Tietz* was officially valued at 300,000 *Reichsmark*, a fraction of its actual worth. They eventually sold the shop and business in November 1938 for an even more paltry 219,400 *Reichsmark*. Even then, the buyers attempted to lower the price, claiming that the cost of removing the ornate facade should be borne by the sellers. The money from the sale was deposited in a blocked account, and it is highly unlikely that the Hirsches could ever have accessed it.

The local newspaper, *Landshuter Zeitung*, by then controlled by the Nazis, reported in November 1938 that, with the department store *Hermann Tietz Nachfolger* turned over to Aryan ownership, the last remaining Jewish-owned business was closed:

Today, this handover to a German family should be understood as a symbolic act: the Landshut economy is now free of Jews.

So, Jews were no longer considered to be German. Where now was the high respect for and popularity of this generous benefactor? Where were those townspeople of Landshut who had appointed Adolf to the civic honour of *Turngemeinde* membership? And how were Adolf and Cilly to survive with no income?

Two years later, the Hirsch home, Villa Hirsch, was similarly expropriated and sold for a small portion of its real value, with the funds placed in a blocked account. The buyer, representing *Deutsche Reichspost* (German Republic Post Office), wrote:

> I want to purchase the property immediately, in order to use it for purposes of the post administration as soon as possible ... – to impose on the Jew, to sell the property within two weeks of delivery of this letter ...

I had to remind myself that I was only learning about the way my family had been robbed – so hard to read about – because the descendants of the perpetrators were determined to face up to the truth, and because a German man, wholly unconnected to me and my family, was spending his days translating texts for me.

Hans had written in an earlier email:

> An email or two ago, you wrote: ' ... and that all through you, Hans ... ' and I must very politely disagree. What made all the difference was you and J coming here and being as forthcoming people as you both are. You would have had all my understanding, had you chosen not to visit Germany,

nor to talk to Germans. What made the difference was that you gave people like Konrad, and all the many others who have answered my requests for information, and myself, the benefit of trust, that Germans today might be different ... You know we can't undo what our parents and grandparents have done in those years. But through such initiatives as the *Stolpersteine*, maybe we might be able to contain the holes that they burned into the fabric of human relations, and maybe even re-knit some of the ends that have come loose.

It is time to leave Wil, and all the friends we've made in Switzerland and Bavaria. Our six-month sojourn is indeed beginning to knit together the holes and loose ends in my understanding of who my father's family were, and this gives me more of a sense of who I am. Previously, I found Germans turned away from me in shame and embarrassment because of the great wrongs that had been done. Now their efforts to reach out to me are helping me towards a sense of belonging, of owning a shared German heritage. I remind myself that England, which accepted my family as refugees in the 1930s, has also committed heinous crimes against other races, building wealth through slavery and colonial genocides. 'He that is without sin among you, let him first cast a stone ... '

Over the next few years, I gather all the memories, files and photos I have accumulated during our house swap to Switzerland. My aim is to assemble a coherent narrative about my father's family, making further enquiries and researching as necessary. Landshut's *Stolpersteine Verein* is subtitled 'Against Forgetting', and I want to set down what I am discovering about the people they were, before these memories are lost again.

A decade after the war ended, Robert's ardent sympathies and Quaker consciousness were engaged over another conflict, the Mau Mau struggle in Kenya. Perhaps he felt shocked by the actions of the country whose proud citizen he had become only seven years previously. The country that had taken him in as a refugee, protecting him and his family from the slaughter of six million of his fellow Jews, was now killing and imprisoning others in their own home country. I was two when he left us.

I sign in to the Asian and African Reading Room in the British Library and contact the Society of Friends for more information about Robert's move to Kenya.

Much has been written about the history of the Mau Mau's fight to gain independence from their white British masters. The needs of the capitalist West were continuing to grow, following the expenses of two world wars and an economic depression all in the space of thirty years. Kenya's fertile uplands had been an attractive prize since its colonial capture at the beginning of the twentieth century. As political scientist Michael Parenti says, poor countries are not 'underdeveloped', they are over-exploited. 'We are here because you were there'; this aphorism coined by the former director of the Institute of Race Relations, Ambalavaner Sivanandan, succinctly explains the ensuing immigration to first-world countries.

The dominant Kikuyu tribe was increasingly resentful of their displacement that was leading to the eradication of the pastoral, itinerant way of life that had preserved land and people for millennia. The Mau Mau – the 'Kenya Land and Freedom Army' – fought for the return of their land, and for autonomy. The British responded with imprisonment in detainment camps, torture, and execution. Mau Mau women were held in separate camps, with the most hardcore punished as 'deviants' in the Kamiti and Gitamayu camps. These women were accused of insanity, and of hurting themselves to cover up injuries inflicted by guards' maltreatment. The government has, in the past decade, paid compensation sums of many millions of pounds to those elderly Kenyans who are still living, but this can never suffice, or recompense the suffering imposed by the British.

The Quakers, as one might expect, did what they could to help the victims. In 1955, they established a Friends Community Centre in Nairobi and the Friends Centre's Church Maringo was co-located there the following year. The Friends Service Council, established in 1927 to carry out the missionary and aid work of British Quakers, reported in their 1956 Yearly Meeting Proceedings that:

> Efforts have been made throughout the year to secure a married couple as wardens of the Quaker community centre in Nairobi, but without avail. Robert Landor, a Macclesfield Friend, offered early in the year to bridge the gap that would be left in Nairobi when Denis Moriarty came home in the spring, and the Kenya Committee gratefully accepted his offer. ... Since the spring Robert Landor has been building up the work of the community centre on the African municipal housing estate of Ofafa.

A librarian at the Society of Friends London office told me that this community centre offered classes in sewing, carpentry, shorthand, literacy and English. The wardens had started a library and a fortnightly film show, working closely with local people. Their aim was to support those black Kenyans who had been displaced to the city from rural areas, and to encourage social cohesion and positive race relations.

The Friends were grappling with the wider implications of these developments, too:

> Meanwhile new life is growing around the temporary centre, which is no more than one of the small African-type houses

next door to those in which our workers and their colleagues live... before long, the population of the estate will have increased considerably – and with it, of course, the scope of our work. There will be much to do, not only in coping with the difficulties of our African neighbours and helping them to settle down to urban life, but indirectly, in trying to study the effects of such urbanisation.

They asked themselves,

Is it a good thing to encourage settlement in the towns and a break from the land and, if so, how can it best be done? If not, what is the alternative? Should the wife be left on the farm, and the husband be encouraged to become merely a migrant labourer?

Those working with Kenyans were beginning to comprehend the value of their traditional way of life:

British Friends are still comparatively new to Kenya. It was not until the Mau Mau insurrection that they became aware, in the fullest sense of the word, that Kenya is a British colony, and that colonisation had resulted in a wholesale disruption of tribal life, of custom and tradition, of morality and the indigenous economy ...

The authors of these newsletters ensured that Quakers across the country could develop an understanding of the underlying moral issues their workers were grappling with in the field.

From the community centre in Nairobi, Robert then joined the relief team working in the Thiba detention camp and surrounding 'resettlement villages'. Their work involved asking the detainees and villagers what kind of help they needed and then trying to provide it. This involved adult literacy groups, women's groups and nursing and midwifery services.

Many years ago, my mother had told me that our father had gone to work in a women's refugee camp in Kenya, after Mau Mau. Until now, that was all I had known. This new information is giving me so much food for thought in my search for the roots from which I sprung. This young man, my father, didn't just talk about helping others. He got involved, he made connections, he listened, and he acted.

Why did Robert feel the need to volunteer? He must have believed that it was not enough to serve others in peacetime England, when people in another country had again been imprisoned in detention camps. His national service in the Scraptoft Prisoner of War camp perhaps led him to see that 'the enemy' comprises many ordinary people like oneself, caught up in a violent spiral not of their volition; this experience might make him useful in a time of reconstruction and rehabilitation. He knew from first-hand experience what conditions in a detention camp could do to a person's mental and physical health. In addition, he would have been aware of the horrifying reports from the troops liberating the Nazi concentration camps in 1945, a decade earlier. At that time, the British public would not have known the full extent of the crimes committed by their government as colonial rulers in Kenya. Nevertheless, his conscience would evidently not permit him to stay on the sidelines.

Once I was a mother of young children myself, I saw this decision in a new light. Previously, I had framed this as the altruistic act of the ardent idealist I knew him to be. Then we began our own family. We used to joke that each new baby needs two parents, and that by having a second, then a third, we had blown that magic ratio. With a houseful of little ones ('peedie breeks' – literally, small trousers – in the Orcadian dialect), there is never enough time, or sleep, and parents feel at the edge of their capacity to cope. Suddenly I saw it as an extraordinarily irresponsible act for Robert to leave behind a young wife and two toddlers, and to travel halfway across the world to a country suffering violent insurrection. Indeed I, his little daughter, had only just recovered from a life-threatening condition. I put this new insight to my mother once when she was visiting us, and she sighed a quiet yes. I suppose he must have asked her to join him, as the centre needed a married couple, but that they had decided he should go first, to check whether it would be safe for a family.

For Margaret, though, I can imagine her dismay at being left behind with their little ones. Perhaps she wondered why they were not enough for him. She once confided to my brother that she had a brief affair with an older family friend at this time; she must have felt desperately abandoned. There seemed to be a generational or cultural chasm between her and her own parents – I remembered her telling me that, as a child, she used to wonder if she had been adopted. It is telling that she turned to (or was preyed upon by?) an older man. Nowadays, we understand that developmentally, a person's sense of identity and belonging are still being formed in early adulthood. Both Robert and Margaret were only in their mid-twenties.

19

FATHERS AND SONS; LETTERS, 1947

What kind of father did Robert want to be? He came into fatherhood only a few years after the difficult time he had had in his relationship with his own father. Looking back at the letters he exchanged with his brother, it is clear that, by Christmas 1947, all was not well between Richard and his children.

In the Goldhurst Terrace two-storey apartment in Swiss Cottage, Stephen and Phyllis lived on one floor, with Richard and Eva on the other. The younger generation re-decorated Richard's living quarters for him. (Some seventy years later, Phyllis gave a scandalised chuckle as she told me they had found a half bottle of whisky in a bookcase, hidden behind Richard's tallest books.) In the months leading up to Robert's twenty-first birthday, he wrote to his brother and sister-in-law, who were hard at work on their PhD theses, about the re-decoration of the Goldhurst Terrace apartment:

> I do feel awfully sorry for you having all this work of your own, and what father wants you to do on top. We did fear something like this would happen.

Robert told them he was 'making an effort to 'get at' Father'. The difference of opinion centred around religious belief on the surface, but also showed the size of the hole their mother's death had left in the fabric of the family:

It is strange that mother's husband is so remote from her
way of thinking and living ...

I find it in my heart to feel sorry for Richard, who had written back
courteously. If he had not fully understood Quakerism, it is perhaps
because his youthful son wrote lengthy explanations in English, a second
language for Richard that he never perfectly grasped. Maybe, also, as a
lifelong agnostic with humanistic principles, he had no personal interest
in religious conversations, aside from a parent's natural wish to engage
with his children's interests.

And yet ... I suppose as adolescents we have all pulled apart our
parents' characters, the failings we perceive in our nearest family
members, but usually this happens in face-to-face discussion. It is a
strange side effect of the war that I can read a twenty-year-old's rants,
preserved for perpetuity in his letters:

> I don't know how frank I can be with him in pointing out
> his own mistakes and failings, not directly but so that he
> realises them from the text. In a very despairing letter of
> yours, Stephen, just before Christmas, you spoke that Father
> failed in life because of Pride, and I certainly think that he
> also has no religion, (I don't necessarily mean formal, but
> in the way Mother had) because of his intellectual pride.

I can hear the hurt of these young men, at the loss of their mother
and their subsequent poor rapport with their father, and I also hear
their youthful arrogant certainty. I am reminded of Turgenev's *Fathers
and Sons*, with its depiction of the dismissive impatience of the sons in
their passionately held opinions, and of the humble unconditionality of
a father's love. Richard had certainly not 'failed in life'. On the contrary,
he was remarkably successful in those pre-Holocaust years, when he

established a thriving business and provided for his growing family. Even after everything he had achieved had been taken from him, he still did his best to provide for them, first by co-managing a department store and then by working in a junior position for the publishing company Allen and Unwin.

Robert referred to Gosse's autobiographical *Father and Son* in one of his letters. The theme of motherlessness is central to the book. Edmund Gosse's mother, who died when he was a child, had been strong, pious, warm and loving towards her child, and had kept the family together. Indeed, she sounds very like Edith. The father stunts his child's development: his son feels like

> ... a plant on which a pot has been placed, with the effect that the centre is crushed and arrested, while shoots are struggling up to the light on all sides ... all [Father] did was to try to straighten the shoots, without removing the pot which kept them resolutely down.

The son is denied the time to be a child and to follow the normal developmental trajectory of childhood. This description seems to mirror the feelings of Richard's sons as they grow towards adulthood.

Robert had sent Richard a booklet with two speeches by Victor Gollancz, because he thought his father 'might be more willing to accept things from this great Jew whom he also admires'. He had a double aim, he claimed:

> ... to improve family relationships by helping him to obtain some kind of understanding for those things, our thoughts which are not contained in his 'philosophy' and, secondly, the only chance of Father being happy is if he surrenders his old being to a certain extent and gains the peace and

tranquillity that he longs for by accepting (without first pulling to pieces and destroying and picking up the bad bits, as is his habit).

So this appears to be at the heart of their difficult relationship – that they felt their father is critical and destructive in his attitude, always 'pulling to pieces', straightening their errant shoots. And so they pull him to pieces in their letters, mirroring their elder's behaviour. To these brothers, who compared that behaviour with how their family had been when their mother was alive, life with Richard must have been hard. Robert had the respite of being away on his national service, and so got out of the decorating, for which he apologised. By March 1948, relationships had further broken down. Stephen and Phyllis were no longer living with Richard, and Robert was wondering what his own action should be after demobilisation.

He wrote:

> For weeks and months, Margaret and I have been discussing this problem, and we have come to two decisions ... that I shall not be living at home during summer. At first I was a bit doubtful about the rightness of this decision, but events during these last two months – Father's treatment of Eva, and the fact that you are now living separately – clinched matters and made me realise that that was the best course to take for the time being. On the other hand, Margaret and I want to make one last – if possible – concerted attack on Father this autumn, last in as much that if we, too, fail, then it will be abundantly clear that nothing can be done with and for Father in his own home – the only other possibility then will be somewhere where he'll not be boss.

Whoa! Having such partial information from only one of the people in a complex and confrontational family situation made it hard for me to know how to align my sympathies. On one hand this very young man, my father-to-be, evoked in me a wry humour when he judged his elderly father with all the arrogance of youth. It reminded me of that self-deprecating Mark Twain quotation:

> When I was a boy of fourteen, my father was so ignorant I could hardly stand to have the old man around. But when I got to be twenty-one, I was astonished at how much the old man had learnt in seven years.

But I could also feel for this particular old man, my grandfather, who had had everything he valued and had achieved in life taken from him, one by one. His children mourned the loss of their mother; how much more must he have missed her? It is easy to believe that he may have been clinically depressed. As I know from experience, this condition leads to having a short fuse, to black-and-white thinking, to an inability to think of anyone else outside one's own black hole. It sounds as if Richard had behaved badly towards Eva, had driven Stephen and Phyllis away and, in short, had somehow made himself impossible to live with. If only Stephen's letters had been preserved as well, to give a rounder picture of events in this family.

And yet, Robert was beginning to show glimmerings of empathy:

> Margaret and I somehow feel, illogically perhaps, that we might yet draw Father out of his dark world of despair and cheerlessness, without too great cost to ourselves ... Quite obviously I cannot tell Father that Margaret and I would rather find digs, and that we want to live at home mainly for his sake ... Anyway, I think it will be best if you don't

mention anything before I come home, as I think Father would prefer if I came straight to him than to hear it from someone else first – you know how he always feels left out of things if we know something about one another before him … . And I think it best to talk about it all early enough to enable him to make plans and know what is going to happen, which again means a lot to Father …

Here was Robert maturing before my eyes! – with the help of his even younger fiancée:

Today's letter contained one very great eye-opener as well, something I had not realised existed in Father to such a great extent, although Margaret has pointed it out to me several times. It came in a passage where he says that, during these last months, he has been fighting the continually recurring impression that, even during absolutely neutral and impersonal subject discussions (I immediately thought of the Van Gogh argument), we condemned his opinion a priori … . It is wrong for someone with hardly any knowledge of psychology to attempt to draw such conclusions in facts, but there we have perhaps Father's greatest trouble: the fact that, since leaving Germany, he has not been appreciated, neither by his children nor by the outer world. Hence during our Van Gogh discussion, his fit of temper and sadness that his own children, quite apart from this country, should doubt the judgement on art of the publisher of the *Delphin-Verlag*. That is why, even during a quiet and reasonable discussion on these things, he is very sad if we do not accept his ideas.

This feels like an accurate analysis. Richard was suffering the long-term effects of bereavement, and of being a powerless refugee in a country that was previously his hated enemy and against whom he had borne arms. He was also holding a menial position as an administrative assistant in a field he had once led. Perhaps he may sometimes have disagreed with decisions or directions taken by his employer, but always had to remain suppliant and grateful. His children were embracing becoming English, which must have felt like a rejection of the cultural heritage that Richard had made his life's work.

The young couple had discussed how to maintain their freedom of thought and action if they were to live with Richard:

> I don't know to what extent she will be able to implement it, but Margaret says that we must be more accommodating on things that do not involve a fundamental principle, not only for the sake of peace, but as his due and for his own peace of mind and happiness. How long she can keep that up, I don't know, but I am rather confident. It is the most difficult thing to keep a balance between helping Father and retaining our personal freedom of thought and action. Any appreciation of Father would not help very much unless it is genuine, and there again that is so much easier for Margaret coming to meet Father fresh and unprejudiced (apart from my evil influence), while I obviously cannot help remembering our previous lives.

I wish I had been able to read these letters while my mother was still alive, so I could have asked her about her memories of this time.

Relationships continued to deteriorate through that summer, with Robert now trying to persuade Stephen to be kinder to their father:

I don't think you realise to what extent Father is completely broken, and what this lack of real friendship, with Eva and lately with you, has meant to him.

Some forty years later, Stephen demonstrated a life-long conflict between his feelings of pride and resentment when he wrote to Dr Schier about Richard. Stephen had begun this letter by explaining that he cannot reply to Dr Schier in German 'as it is fifty-five years since I wrote a letter in German', but that he can read and understand her letter with no problems. When learning a new language, I know as a former EFL teacher that it is best to learn in this order: listening before speaking, reading before writing. It seems that losing a birth language follows the same rules, but in reverse.

Stephen wrote:

My father was a highly gifted man. He wrote plays and sketches, poems and outstanding letters ... He volunteered for the Imperial German Army, fought on the Russian Front and later on the Western Front as a lieutenant and was awarded decorations. ... despite the Depression, [he] developed it [*Delphin-Verlag*] into a highly successful publishing business ... He was what we call in England a Victorian ... a strict disciplinarian who rather frightened his children. ... he was proud of being the first publisher in Germany on Picasso, philosophy and modern literature. However, when I was old enough to know him, he was a very difficult man to live with, having lost his life's work, his exceptionally loving and gifted wife ... and in some ways, his children, because they were growing up English.

It is not hard to understand Richard's low state in 1947 when he was sixty-five years old. He had made a good living and established a successful business through his passion for modern art and culture. He had lived in a beautiful home in the city, country and language he revered, with a loving wife and growing family. Little by little he had lost every single thing he held dear. In other circumstances, he might have been edging towards retirement and a life of leisure, to enjoy his interests, in good health, with sufficient means and his family around him. Yet all this was gone, and his children were growing away from him.

Added to this catalogue of grieving were the typical problems of ageing. Evolution prioritises the transmission of healthy genes to secure the survival of the species. Once their reproductive days are over, older individuals in a social species may still have a role in transmitting wisdom and helping nurture the young, but their declining powers mean they will eventually become a burden on the group. Mental faculties, senses, physical health and strength all diminish on a trajectory that will only end in death. As Richard's children took their places in the world, I think he felt superfluous, and with some courage, took himself back to Germany to live out his remaining time.

Between Richard's return to Bavaria in 1954 and his death in 1960, Robert had taken us to meet our grandfather, but Eva and Stephen had not visited him. The rift between the father and his two elder children had not been repaired. If this was a Hollywood film, It's a Wonderful Life or Carousel, things would be different. A guardian angel would oversee all this family misunderstanding and distress and help them to sort it out, with a judicious bit of cloud-break viewing of past and future and a word in their ear. I have been granted this glimpse into their lives, but am powerless to do anything – except bear witness.

20

TRAUMA AND RESILIENCE; REFLECTION

The two older Landauer children, Eva and Stefan, had borne the brunt of the growing anti-Semitism of the mid-1930s. My father, Robert, would have been less aware of what was developing, being only six years old in 1933. He may also have been protected by his own sunny character traits.

A combination of protective factors, some external, some internal, forges resilience in an individual. After Bowlby's and Ainsworth's laboratory-based research into child development in the 1960s, psychologists in the next decade recognised the importance of the multi-layered contexts that surround the child. These generate complex interactions at every level. As every parent knows, each child in the family is born with personality traits that are different to their siblings'. The parents' genes throw up a different combination each time, making each of their babies unique. Our first child was a calm baby, ready with a smile for a familiar adult but also happy with his own company. Every time he awoke, sounds of exploratory play and contented vocalisations drifted from the baby monitor. I was looking forward to repeating this experience when our second child was born two years later, and was taken aback by how different this new baby was – in physique, in character, in sociability. He looked for people and company from the very start, and I had to learn how to be a different kind of mother. When we had a third child, insensitive acquaintances commented in front of our two little boys how glad I must be to have a girl at last. I tried to explain that there couldn't be any greater difference than already existed between the two older children.

Each baby's innate characteristics affect how that infant relates to their environment, and to the people in their immediate context, which in turn affects how these others respond to them. Bronfenbrenner, an American psychologist, proposed an 'onion-layer', ecological model: the circle surrounding the child – the 'microsystem', made up of family, school and friends – interacts with the surrounding layers, or 'macrosystem', of neighbourhood, social media, socioeconomic status, culture and so on. These interactions are all contextualised with the passing of time.

To understand this in the context of my father's family, each of the three Landauer children had different experiences at critical times in their development during the 1930s, those traumatic years of fast-moving change. Eva was born at the start of her parents' marriage, when Richard was building up a successful publishing business. Born a precise nine months after their wedding, one can imagine her parents' delight at beginning their next generation in whom they could invest all their dreams for the future. Eva was ten when they were forced to leave Munich, to live above her grandparents' department store. Stefan was eight and Robert was six. In terms of a child's understanding, there are tremendous gaps between those ages. Their childhood photos show their distinct personalities, which determine how other people would relate to each of them: Eva looks contained and artistic, Stefan thoughtful and sensitive, whereas Robert looks cheerful and outgoing. The complex interplay of ecological context and individual characteristics affected the capacity of each one to withstand the adverse experiences they were going through, with resultant lifelong implications. Eva suffered from periodic mental breakdowns throughout her life. Stefan hid his German beginnings from his own family, unable to discuss it at all.

When his widow was apprised of her children's involvement in our visit to Landshut to explore our Landauer roots, she was clear that their father would have hated it and begged them to go no further. My father, Robert, on the other hand, made efforts to keep up with his own father after Richard had returned to Bavaria, introduced us to our elderly German relatives in London, and supported our mother, Margaret, to become the 'keeper' of Landauer artefacts and history.

Eva Maria   *Stefan Klaus*   *Robert Felix*
Landauer 1922-88   *Landauer 1925-2013*   *Landauer 1927-86*

Eva's school-friend, Frau Erika Stadler, had been too frail to attend our civic ceremony in Landshut, but among those attending in a private capacity was her representative – perhaps a relative, neighbour or carer – who introduced herself in order to pass Erika's greetings on to me. Erika had written to my mother in 1997, when Margaret was planning a trip to Landshut, giving details of the historic wedding pageant re-enactment and the local amenities. The visit never took place, but it felt special to have this link with my aunt, Eva, through this contact from her oldest friend.

I thought back to 1959, to the time when we lived with Eva in the family flat in Goldhurst Terrace, London, in the few months between our three-year stints in Kenya and Ghana.

'Are you awake? May I get into bed beside you?'

'Of course, my little pussycat.'

When I was little, Eva always called me her pussycat. I realise now, as I didn't then, that *Kätzchen* (pussycat) is a common term of endearment in German. Perhaps Eva had been her own mother's little *Kätzchen*. As a weekend early morning treat, I would snuggle into bed beside my aunt. She always listened to the BBC Third Programme, with its feast of classical music, on days when she didn't have to go to work. Many Jewish refugees had found their career and professional home in the BBC during the war and in the decades that followed; perhaps their familiar European accents, as well as the music of her homeland and her upbringing, were a comfort to Eva. She gave us her grand piano a few years later, when she had to leave the Goldhurst Terrace apartment to move to a smaller flat. She was a proficient pianist, and that must have been a wrench for her, an additional loss of the person she once had been.

Some years later, when I was studying for my Postgraduate Certificate in Education in 1975 and living with J in Battersea, I made an effort to reconnect with my aunt. My last visit to her shocked me. By then she was living in a far smaller flat than the Goldhurst Terrace family home, above a narrow traffic-filled channel of a road in Archway. Every door and window had a massive hasp and padlock on it, evidencing her terror of intruders. Although only in her early fifties, she was thin and stooped, wearing a long, dark cardigan and skirt, with her lifeless hair scraped into a little bun. She wanted to be a good host and fed me an evening meal, despite eating nothing herself, and provided an unidentifiable pie, a tomato and a few biscuits on a small plate. These oddments were soft, stale, and barely edible. As she brought the plate through, I caught a glimpse into the room behind her; even the kitchen cupboards had heavy staples and locks affixed. Being young, I didn't know how to comment or to question her. Now I wish I had.

Nevertheless, that evening we had an enjoyable discussion about literature, the subject of my first degree. Eva seemed to approve of how her little pussycat was turning out.

'Well done with the English degree.'

'Thank you. It was a desperate rush in the final year to get through everything. There was such a lot to read!'

'I don't know how you did it. I read so slowly; it takes me forever just to get through one poem. But I do love poetry,' she said, pointing at the thin volumes in the bookcase by her chair.

I explained that I was a fast reader and couldn't take the time to appreciate the way every word counts in a poem. As I told her, I preferred to rattle through Victorian novelists such as Dickens, skimming as I read, and not bothering to master names of characters or places – a handicap when it came to exams. We traded our favourite authors with each other, marvelling at our differences.

At last, the conversation wound down, and Eva brought through an armful of bedding. Together we made up a mattress with cushions from the sofa and chair.

'I'll show you the bathroom. Once you've used it, I'll have to lock your door, so make sure you do everything you need to now … '

Eva's voice was quiet but resolute; I did not feel able to argue or even to discuss this strange instruction. Once locked in the sitting room, sleep became impossible, as I felt a strengthening urge to go to the toilet again, triggered by my strange meal.

I lay there in some discomfort, remembering a similar episode from my childhood. When we lived in Kenya in the 1950s, my parents liked to take us on excursions to see the nature and prehistory of the country. We made day trips where possible but had overnight stays if necessary.

On one occasion when I was four or five, we were staying in a small cabin in the bush, with an outside toilet. My parents had been invited out for the evening, perhaps for a game-viewing excursion.

'Now that you've been to the lav, we're going to lock the cabin door. You mustn't go outside on your own, because of the lions,' our father said sternly. Indeed, we could hear an occasional roaring in the distance.

He had already accompanied me across the backyard to the latrine shed, but the moment I was tucked up next to my brother, I knew I needed to go again. The usual argument ensued, with my mother pleading clemency on my behalf and my father attempting to maintain consistency of authority. I am sure I got taken back to the shed, but that panicked feeling of urgency for a toilet when unable to access one may never leave me. On this occasion in Eva's sitting room, I resorted to the humiliating expedient of tissues and a bag. The situation weighed heavily on me; Eva was locking terror out, but I felt panic at being locked in.

There is no longer anyone alive of that generation to ask, but I wonder now about this label of 'schizophrenia' for Eva. All the locks pointed to an acute feeling of danger and persecution – surely irrational in an upper storey flat in Archway – and paranoia is a well-known symptom of schizophrenia.

And yet ... Eva had been persecuted. During her adolescence, a time when forming an independent identity is the foremost developmental task, her life had indeed been in great danger. She was forbidden to meet her friend Erika. Even passing notes in that basket hauled up on a string must have felt very dangerous for the two girls, whose friendship the Nazi authorities had forbidden. Again, it came to me: the body remembers trauma, and we need very little to trigger a freeze, fight or flight response.

Erika Stadler remembered her lovingly all through the long years. When Eva died at Stephen's Devon home in December 1988, fifty

years after they'd last seen each other, Erika placed this notice in the
Landshuter Zeitung:

> Miss Eva Maria Landor, formerly Landauer emigrated in 1938.
> Our dear schoolmate ... after a difficult and bravely endured
> fate, she left this life in Devon, England and awakened to
> a better one. All who knew and loved her will gather for a
> memorial service on Saturday, 14 January at 10 a.m. in Thekla
> Church. May God now give her the joys that were denied
> her on earth. In silent mourning, the Ursuline Absolvia
> class of 1938.

Eva came to my wedding the summer after I'd visited her, a shrunken
woman looking far older than her years. How brave she was! It feels
important to honour her courage, and to have told a little about the
stumbling stones in her life.

21

A FRAGMENTED CHILDHOOD; REFLECTION

Because of my itinerant childhood, I know more national anthems than most, each redolent of its era and mindset. The tune I picked out when I first encountered a piano was God Save The Queen, which in my childhood was still played at each film showing in cinemas. I think my favourite, though, was the Guyanese anthem of around 1966, as it lauded the beauties of nature, rather than nationalist symbols of state:

> Dear land of Guyana, of rivers and plains,
> Made rich by the sunshine and lush by the rains,
> Set gem-like and fair between mountains and sea,
> Your children salute you, dear land of the free.

Typical Pepsicola-coloured creek, Guyana; Reni

'Belonging' is now one of the indicators schools measure when trying to improve pupils' wellbeing and behaviour. Children feel they belong when their culture and language, knowledge and community are affirmed by others in their everyday lives – when they feel accepted for who they are. Being secure, both in their identity and in their community, helps a child to respect and relate to others, to feel connected. Perhaps that is the purpose of a national anthem – to give a sense of belonging. Does it still work, when the experience of learning a new national anthem is repeated again and again, as it was when I moved from country to country? Being a third culture kid adds layers of complexity to the concept of belonging; the family unit is the only constant, but not much time is spent together.

Panbros Beach, Ghana, Christmas 1961; Margaret, author, friends

After Ghana, we lived in our house in Ashbourne for a few years, during my sister's first years of life.

I attended the local PNEU school, where the curriculum and pedagogy hadn't changed from its genesis in colonial days; the Parents' National Educational Union had been created to deliver a classical English education, through home tuition by parents living in countries where there was no school. We took turns to read aloud from textbooks, closed the book and narrated what we had just read. At the start of the next lesson, we narrated what we had retained from the previous day – often very little. *From Ur to Rome* was particularly dry. We kept century books, laying out events on a timeline from prehistory to the present day, and splodged watercolour paint in messy attempts at portraying wildflowers in our nature books. These were thick, A4 hardback volumes. It was expected we would maintain similar notebooks throughout our lives, like well-brought-up ladies. The timetable included lessons in art and music appreciation, Shakespeare, Old and New Testament, French and Latin, as well as English and maths, geography and history; but there was no science for us. The two women who ran the school, Miss Mulliner and Miss Jones, who seemed very elderly to us, tried at one stage to deliver a few science lessons. I remember standing in a circle around Miss Mulliner, teacher of the top class, as she dissected a bull's eye on the kitchen table, and then measured the boiling point of oil on the Aga. Both experiments ended in disaster, as wailing children contended with streams of vomit and leaping flames. Science lessons were never again attempted.

Caravan dwelling, Fenny Bentley, whilst awaiting renovation of house 1961;
Robert, Margaret, author, Mark

Then I passed the eleven plus, and, the only one from that school to do so, started at Queen Elizabeth Grammar School, in the days when secondary education was selective. My fellow PNEU pupils continued to be educated in private schools. I felt like a square peg in a round hole; my accent was wrong – too posh – and I knew no one. However, some of the teachers who had taught my mother spoke kindly to me, and a few of the girls befriended me. I began to settle in. After a couple of weeks, the headteacher came into our classroom and spoke quietly to the teacher at the front. Then he told me to collect my belongings and accompany him to a new class. This was a second-year class. Evidently my educational progress had led them to believe it would be better to move me up a year. I was devastated. I had only just begun to make friends and now had to begin all over again. I couldn't help crying, and indeed I cried the whole day. I could see my new classmates and teacher looking concerned, but I could do nothing to stop the tears. Looking back, it was perhaps the best thing I could have done to be accepted – I was so obviously not crowing over my success. Quite quickly, I was adopted by my peers and loved my time there, enjoying friendly academic competition and the company of kind boys as well as girls.

The Mount, Ashbourne, pirate party, 1962; Mark, friends

The following Easter, after only two terms there, my parents moved me to a boarding school in York. In the space of less than a year, this was my fourth set of classmates, and it proved too much for me. I never fitted in and was homesick and bullied. I was able to hold my own academically, except in science where, by skipping first year, I had missed the necessary foundation, but I had poor physical coordination. Daily sports lessons were torture. 'Can't you run backwards, Miriam?' they sneered every tennis lesson, except that they had corrupted my name to a bad word, so that even my identity was a source of shame. And no, I couldn't run backwards. Decades later, I was diagnosed with hypermobility, which explains my poor balance and coordination. I spent three and a half years there – ten long school terms.

I left boarding school after O-levels, when my parents at last noticed how unhappy I was, and switched to Derby Technical College to begin my A-levels. After only two terms I went to Brussels as an au pair to 'improve my French', one of my A-level subjects; my parents were leaving England again, for a six-month posting to Geneva. The following year, at a residential sixth-form college in Oxford, the Parisian *assistante* used to choose me to read out loud so she could snigger at my Belgian accent.

During those years of my secondary education, Robert moved from post to post, from Guyana, to New York, to Geneva and then to Zambia. At boarding school, I was bullied and unhappy, but in other places I made friends and prospered.

The feeling of not belonging, of being fragmented, can lead to some dark emotions. As a teenager I had confessed to my father a childish misdeed that had happened several years previously. My crime was this: when we lived for a while in my mother's hometown of Ashbourne, she had sent me shopping to her aunt's haberdashery to buy a card of elastic. It was a fine summer's day as I crossed the cobbled marketplace, looking around me at the busy stalls. The coin I'd been given was not enough, but Auntie Elsie gave me the elastic anyway.

'Your mum needs this now? Take it, ducks. She can pop in with the extra pennies next time she's passing.'

Jones Beach, New York 1968; author, Robert, Reni

Auntie Elsie spoke with a Derbyshire accent, as did all my maternal relatives – 'moom', 'doocks', 'passing' with a short A. Somewhere along the way my mother had learnt to speak in RP, the Received Pronunciation of the BBC, which accentuated my feeling of us not fitting into Ashbourne life. I forgot to tell 'Moom' on my return home. By the time I remembered, some days later, I was too embarrassed to own up. I had robbed my own great-aunt, and felt black shame every time I thought of it.

When I finally came clean to my dad, he laughed and shared with me his own experience of childhood remorse. His family had lived in a flat in Fitzroy Square in their first years in London, following their arrival in 1938. At that time, it was a poor, rundown neighbourhood. The local greengrocer was kind to the two young refugee boys, and Robert and his older brother used to help shift the vegetable boxes on Saturday mornings. My cheeky dad, as a joke, held out his hand –

'Where's my pay?' The greengrocer, perhaps understanding it was a joke or perhaps not, gave him a ha'penny. Robert felt similar black shame at this memory. We absolved each other, and laughed wryly at the passions of childhood, which are too black and heavy to be admitted to at the time.

I realise now that guilt is for something you did, and its absolution is forgiveness. Shame, on the other hand, is for who you are, and the only antidote is grace, acceptance. And humiliation is an exercise of power to induce feelings of shame in another person. Our shamed reaction to these childish misdemeanours was telling. Parenting practices that focus on strict discipline use humiliation to eradicate whatever is seen as unacceptable behaviour, potentially leaving a lifelong legacy of feelings of unworthiness. My father's philosophy of child-rearing, mirroring his own upbringing by his elderly German father, was to be very strict in our early years, using sarcasm and spanking as tools. Once we had internalised an understanding of right and wrong, there would be no need of further discipline, he believed. My mother, on the other hand, understood child development better, and tailored her expectations to the limitations of a small child's abilities in self-regulation. I remember feeling frightened of my father when I was very young, although he later became my best ally. Perhaps, though, harsh parenting in those first years, which is a critical time of development, had left both father and daughter with a propensity to believe any inadvertent mistake was proof of our inherent otherness, of not belonging, leading us to feel shame instead of guilt.

Even though he was the disciplinarian in our family, Robert was also the one who could understand and forgive one's most shameful feelings. I was desperately jealous of my brother on his first return from boarding school, as my mother showered him with treats 'to make up for what he'd missed'. I protested that she had given me none of these in his absence. My father's sympathetic listening and unconditional love got me over this period. When I rebelled against homework, stating defiantly that I would prefer to just get married and have children, he explained he had married my mother because of, not despite, her educational achievement. I grew up surrounded by these aesthetic and moral foundations.

I was only in my early thirties when Robert died, almost forty years ago. He has been missing from my life for longer than the time I had with him. I think I'm still looking for him.

I felt an instant sense of connection when my husband and I moved to Orkney in 1980. When we first arrived, we were given a key worker's house in Stromness. This small town, whose main street meanders along parallel to the shoreline, is criss-crossed by closes. These are small, steep alleyways running up the side of Brinkie's Brae, the hill on which Stromness is built, linking the main arterial routes through the town. Ashbourne has the same network of little passages, which I loved to explore as a child. Then, my progress would be halted by old ladies, enquiring gently but persistently as to my genealogy: 'You'll be Nan's granddaughter? No? Then her great-niece? So – you must be Mabel's ... ' and so it continued, until I was placed precisely within the framework of Ashbourne families. I found that the older folk in Stromness carried out a similar mining for credentials, with patient, indirect questioning, but with no conclusion to the conversation until the enquirer had satisfied their curiosity. The unspoken assumption was that you belonged, and it was just a matter of working out in what way. It made me feel quite at home.

If a newcomer arrives in Orkney by sea they are known as a 'ferrylouper' – one who has jumped off, 'louped', from the ferry, as we did. Those who arrive by plane are treated to this safety announcement about locating the nearest exit: '...bearing in mind that it may be behind you.' As I work on discovering who I am, I realise I must trace some long roots into what is behind me, before I can loup forward to plant myself in the present.

Orkney from a plane

My father too must have had to work hard on who he now wanted to be; as Judith Kerr wrote in *A Small Person Far Away*, 'Since the Nazis came, we haven't belonged in any place, only with refugees like ourselves.' Robert had been granted British nationality in 1949, but perhaps he found a sense of belonging still eluded him, leading him to take up this fragmented career that involved so many workplaces and countries – and committing his children to fragmented childhoods, mirroring his own.

22

LOSING THE OLDER
GENERATION; REFLECTION

I am thinking myself back into a childhood memory, from August 1960, when I was seven. Our family were home on summer leave from Ghana, at our new home, The Mount in Ashbourne. Mark was away somewhere with our father. I was lying in bed, following the rows of tiny white dots on the baby-blue wallpaper – up and down, side to side, diagonally. My parents chose this design for their little girl with love, but its pattern drove me mad in those endless hours before sleep came. Another trick I'd learnt to pass the time was to stare at the crack of light along the closed door from the landing outside my bedroom. I could make this pencil-thin line separate into two light strips, widening and dissolving back together again in a flowing dance, by staring very hard. The previous year, in Accra, I had spent these long hours before sleep watching the traffic lights twinkling in the far distance, red, red and amber, green, amber, red. Only now does it occur to me that traffic lights don't twinkle – there must have been trees in-between. What a leap from the airless sweat of humid Accra to the cool summer nights of Derbyshire; the wakefulness was the same, however.

Then I heard the phone ring in the hall below. Who could this be? In our family, and in this era, we only used phones for brief messages of necessity, for emergencies, or bad news. I tiptoed onto the landing and crouched by the banisters, straining to hear, but could make no sense of what I heard.

'Yes, that's right ... He's not here just now ... Oh no. How dreadful ... Have you told the others? ... Yes ... Thank you for telling me.' Her voice sounded shocked and sombre as she finished the call.

191

I shifted my head to lean on the wooden uprights and a small creak gave me away. My mother came raging up the stairs, emotion released in scolding:

'You're not supposed to get out of bed! Why aren't you asleep? You have school tomorrow! It's really late ... '

I ran back to bed, asking in a scared tone what the phone call was about. I learnt that my German Jewish grandfather – who had survived two world wars, the Nazis, the premature death of his adored wife, and the loss of his country, home and livelihood – my grandfather had died. He had been knocked down by a car when crossing the road near his home, where it bends to go into the underpass, making a blind corner. Was this why I recognised the underpass, decades later? Had his spirit somehow infused the environs with meaning for me? His deafness meant he hadn't heard the car approaching and he had stepped out in front of it. That night I cried myself to sleep, not so much for the grandfather I barely knew but for my father, who was now an orphan.

When my brother hears about this memoir, he remembers that among our mother's effects are her school certificates and teaching references, and sends them to me. Here is proof, if any were needed, of her ability. She had earned seven credits and two 'very goods' on her school certificate, from Ashbourne's august Queen Elizabeth Grammar School. The University of Birmingham Institute of Education, certifying her approved course of study at Leicester Training College, had awarded her distinction and credit among her further qualifications.

As I read through all her references, it hits me for the first time that, just as my education had been disrupted by so many moves, so too had my mother's career; she followed her husband around the world, and brought up three children. Her first teaching post had been in the Connaught County Secondary School in Leytonstone, which she left only a month before my brother's birth. While Robert worked in the Friends Refugee clinic in Kenya, Margaret was volunteering at the Bollington Spastic Clinic (now called cerebral palsy) in Cheshire. She taught English and art at the Duchess of Gloucester High School for Asian girls while we lived in Nairobi. I remember sometimes waiting for her in the staff room there, cooed over by the secretaries who let me play with their stationery. On the school's open days, I stuffed myself with delicious Indian sweetmeats that were drenched in fragrant syrups.

During our six-month stay with Eva in London in 1959, my mother taught then too, at the Starcross School in Grey's Inn Road. Margaret took on private coaching in Ghana, preparing students for the School Leavers Certificate. She didn't work for several years after my sister Reni was born, and was a stay-at-home mother in Guyana (1966–7) and in New York (1967–8). In Zambia (1969–72) she worked four days a week in the Curriculum Development Centre, 'Zambianising' educational material for schools. Robins and snowmen had little relevance to a Zambian child, and she used to read out loud to us her English-language versions of local folk tales. She was a talented writer and made the stories come alive whilst using the simplest words.

After that, my father had a spell of teaching at Swansea University, on a development course for mature overseas students; Margaret was again a stay-at-home mother, while my sister attended a local primary school. Then while Robert had a post in Birmingham, she worked at the Steward Street Reception Centre, teaching English as a second language. Her last post, teaching English as an additional language at Littleover School near Derby, was the longest period of continuous work in her whole life; she worked there from 1975 until 1987, the year after Robert's death. Her tally of eight teaching posts over forty years still falls short of the ten schools I attended during my childhood, but certainly doesn't follow the ladder-climbing progression of a typical professional career.

It was nevertheless clear that Margaret was well regarded by her employers. Her reference from the Duchess of Gloucester School in Nairobi read:

> The teaching of English to girls to whom it is a foreign language needs great skill and patience, and Mrs Landor has shown that she can adapt her approach in teaching to meet these needs.

As I read, I think about her own circumscribed upbringing in a small town in Derbyshire, where she can't have met many foreigners, and I feel proud to be her daughter: '... good teacher ... friendly and encouraging ... genuine personal interest in each ... ' Perhaps daughters often wish they had known more about their mothers, appreciated them as women as well as mothers, whilst there was still time.

After she retired, Margaret dabbled in a few interests. She tried running Green Hall Cottage as a Bed and Breakfast, but gave that up almost immediately. She kept a few Jacob sheep to spin and knit their wool; we all have scratchy socks from that time. Then she wanted to live nearer to children and grandchildren and sold her house in Ashbourne, moving to Essex where my siblings lived. Following a hysterectomy, she rented a winter-let cottage in Orkney, enabling her to build up a relationship with her grandchildren here. She loved Orkney in the winter and formed the habit of spending some months in a rented cottage near us every year.

Once when she was snowed in, I phoned to check she had enough food.

'Of course I have, but I've run out of film!' she snapped – a far worse disaster. She had begun to take her art more seriously; she sat her A-level then passed her foundation year at art college.

Margaret had just embarked on a full art degree when her ovarian cancer returned. This had been treated by the hysterectomy seven years previously, and she didn't tell us, her children, about the results of her annual check-ups, so we had assumed all was well. Now metastasis was diagnosed, and she died quickly, at the too-young age of seventy-one. She still had so much she planned to do.

When Robert was dying, fourteen years earlier, she was the primary carer, and we children were rather shut out. I think she couldn't cope with our feelings on top of her own. But by the time she was living what turned out to be her last few weeks, she allowed us to help. My brother, Mark, converted a garden room into a bedroom for her so she could leave hospital and be at the heart of his young family. My sister, Reni, lived nearby, and we came down from Orkney to be with her. The three of us, her children, took turns to sit with her, day and night. Macmillan nurses came twice a day, looking after the medical aspects of catheters and morphine drips, reassuring us all with their calm kindness. At the time I felt only a blur of unspoken incomprehension and denial; I couldn't cope with experiencing or expressing difficult emotions.

As a child and teenager, I must have harboured subconscious fear and resentment at being abandoned, repeatedly during my first year of life and then again during those ten terms I spent at boarding school, but without allowing any anger against my mother to surface. I couldn't afford the luxury of adolescent rebellion. I was only at home for brief spells, after the age of twelve, and needed these to be happy times. I had that dislocated feeling of being a third culture kid, constantly on the move, who didn't belong anywhere. My delayed and deeply buried emotions slowly worked their way out during my adulthood, and our relationship swung from closeness to irritation many times. I felt bludgeoned when she died.

In 1986 my mother had arranged the funeral for my father, but now, fourteen years later, we middle-aged children had to step forward to organise one for her. Mark and Reni sat with me in the funeral director's office, being asked to make countless minuscule decisions: which was her favourite piece of music; who would speak; how many cars we would need; even what font to use on the printed programme. It felt so strange to be the ones in charge.

Left on our own for a moment, I confided to my siblings,

'I'm feeling like I've done really well so far, but now I'd like the grown-ups to come back and take over again.'

My brother smiled his understanding, but my sister said in a surprised tone,

'You *are* the grownups!'

For her, a decade younger than us, she could still feel sheltered. But in my mind, we were suddenly the older generation, the holders of all our family knowledge. There was no one left to ask about the past, or the way our family did things.

And in the seriousness of that realisation, I felt a sudden unprecedented pride as I thought: 'I *am* 'just like my mother'! I can be strong, and support others through illness and even death. I can say yes to adventures anywhere in the world, and make family life work in another culture. I can experience different food, tastes, smells. I can embark on new learning, new careers, new interests – expanding my life, not diminishing it.' As she did, throughout her life.

It has been an unexpected gift to get to know my father as a young man through his letters, with this journey of discovery triggered by the chance meeting with Hans. And now it has been wonderful to get to know another side of my mother, and to understand her life a little better. I am beginning to knit together.

23

DISCOVERING *DELPHIN-VERLAG*; LONDON, 2015

While I am getting to know the young Robert through his letters, I receive another gift. My beloved brother-in-law, Andrew, a former librarian, discovers that there is a cache of *Delphin-Verlag* books held by the Warburg Institute in London. With Andrew's help, I contact the chief librarian there and we secure an appointment, to discuss the collection and to see the books for ourselves.

Born in 1866, Aby Warburg was one of five sons of a wealthy Jewish banking family in Hamburg. He gave up his share of the family business in exchange for his brothers' commitment to buy him whatever books he requested. In this way, he was able to establish a library, which later became a research institute, specialising in his unique vision of cross-disciplinary historical, philological and anthropological culture. His own research work, culminating in the unfinished *Bilderatlas Mnemosyne* (remembrance picture atlas) focused on the transmission of culture across the ages. Warburg's enormous collection of books and photographs was categorised and housed according to his own system: Image (first floor), Word (second floor), Orientation (third floor) and Action (fourth floor). He died in 1929, the year of the Wall Street crash, as the economy collapsed and censorship of art, culture and knowledge began to take hold in Germany. The entire library was transferred from Hamburg to London in 1933, when the Nazi persecution of Jewish-owned organisations was at its height and books were being burnt in Berlin. The Warburg Institute is now part of the University of London and is housed in Woburn Square, Bloomsbury.

Andrew and I visit on a crisp winter day. The librarian explains to us that, because the Warburg Institute is not now renowned for art, but rather for history and anthropology, their collection of *Delphin-Verlag* books is not as much sought by researchers as many others in their collection. This means that most of the books we are interested in are still in pristine condition and readily available for our viewing. We find eighty-six *Delphin-Verlag* titles in the library catalogue. Warburg had purchased some of these to add to his collection in the years before his death, but others were acquired in 1961 and are labelled 'Landauer bequest' as their provenance. This is something I must find out about.

We are escorted to the first floor to look at the 'Image' category, with a print-out of the catalogue of *Delphin-Verlag* books in our hands. Scanning the shelves, it is easy to find first one, then more and more. After sampling a few at random, I settle down to a structured search,

camera in hand. I plan to make a personal record of every single volume in the Warburg collection that my grandfather had published.

The range of his books is extraordinary. Each is individually designed and exquisitely produced. At the top end of the range are thick volumes like *Otto Wagner: eine Monographie* by Joseph August Lux. Published in 1914, this has a gold-tooled leather spine, leather covered corners and an abstract marbled design in dark, earth colours on the cover.

Otto Wagner: eine Monographie (Otto Wagner: a Monograph)

Others have richly patterned fabric covers.

It is interesting to see that the dolphin logo changes several times during the life of *Delphin-Verlag*. I remember that Richard's younger cousin Walter Landor (Landauer) had pioneered branding and

Münchener Landschafter (Munich landscapes)

image techniques in his international, California-based company. It seems that my grandfather too had a good eye for design.

Examples of change in logo design

My favourites are the little books, *Kleine Delphin-Kunstbücher*, each slightly bigger than our familiar Ladybird books; these had been launched in this format some twenty years before the Ladybirds. Richard's aim was to make art and culture accessible to everyone, so he produced

the *Kleine Delphin-Kunstbücher* as cheaply as possible. Nevertheless, each one is still individually designed and contains many black-and-white illustrations and photos. I buy several of these following my Warburg visit, and I value them highly.

Because Warburg's Image collection is less frequented than other sections of the library, as we were told, several of the *Delphin-Verlag* books still have the marketing fliers inserted. The

Some of the Kleine Bucher (Little Books) series

librarian says that these leaflets are now collectors' items in their own right.

Marketing flier

Others have the publisher's own notes of dates and prices inscribed, adding to their collector value:

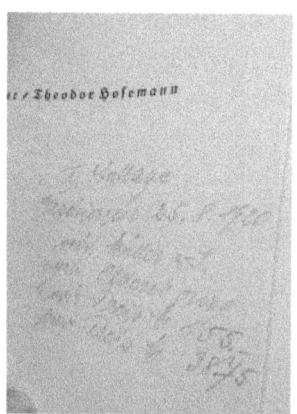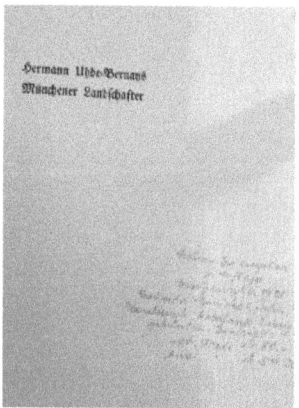

Publisher's notes

Richard's German patriotism during the First World War is evidenced by the series *Unsere Feinde* (Our enemies); subtitles are *Wie sie die Deutschen hassen / wie sie sich selber loben / wie sie einander lieben* (How they hate the Germans / praise themselves / love each other). What bitter irony that a mere two decades later, these compatriots took his publishing firm from him, people of the Jewish race no longer being considered German.

Unsere Feinde (Our Enemies) series

The books that affect me most deeply are those containing a bookplate that reads:

PRESENTED BY HIS CHILDREN
IN MEMORY OF
DR RICHARD LANDAUER
FOUNDER AND OWNER OF *DELPHIN-VERLAG*

These are the books from his publisher's archive, which Richard brought with him from Germany to London. They are not, of course, all the books that *Delphin-Verlag* published, but perhaps were his favourites, or the ones he hoped might interest an English readership. After his death, his children must have decided that this collection should be kept together and held by an appropriate research institute, hence their bequest to the Warburg Library. I feel moved that despite ruptures to their relationship with their father, they wanted to record their pride in his life's achievement with this book plate.

The realisation that these books must have been stored in the Landauers' Goldhurst Terrace flat, where I had lived briefly when I was six, brought memories flooding back. For a few months, I had lived as part of an extended family whose culture was rooted in art, literature and music. I might have touched these very books.

The more I immerse myself in the story of my father's family, the more I want to bear witness to as much of their experience as I can. On my next visit to London, I 'Citymapper' my way to Parsifal Road in West Hampstead. This is the address cited on the Landshut deregistration document, where Cilly's widowed sister, Rose Peiser, lived with her three daughters, Irene, Lilli and Hilde. I read Lilli Palmer's evaluation of their house in her autobiography *Change Lobsters and Dance*. Her family call it 'the second ugliest house in London, bearing in mind the remote possibility that there might be one uglier,' she wrote. I wander down a wide, car-lined street, with large terraced and semi-detached houses set back from the pavement, whose purchase would now set you back some millions of pounds. They built these houses in the 1890s, as new train lines and stations were being constructed. Wide steps lead up to the half-windowed front door of the Peiser family's former abode, through which I can see a generously proportioned hallway stretching back through the building. I ring the doorbell and wait, hoping to enquire about its history from the inhabitants, but no one is home. I love the house. Lilli's idea of ugliness differed greatly from mine, or else the intervening decades have wrought radical change. I imagine my father's family feeling a mixture of grief and relief as Aunt Rose and her daughters welcome them.

In another instance of the serendipitous connections that are guiding my journey of discovery, Andrew comes up with additional information. He has done some more research unbeknownst to me, and has discovered a file named 'Dr Richard Landauer' in the Allen and Unwin publisher archive held by Reading University. Their database shows letters from 1940 onwards, and some reader reports written by Richard. Further correspondence with the university librarian leads to her sending me copies of another pack of letters, this time between Stanley Unwin, his secretary and my grandparents, Edith and Richard. The first letter is dated 10 September 1940, on headed letter paper; now I have their second address in London to check out, in Fitzroy Square.

Edith had written a request for help, politely and in fairly good English, to 'Allen and Unwin Publisher':

> Excuse me to bother you with this letter. My husband, Dr Richard Landauer, was interned two months ago with others of category C.

During the 'fifth column' scare following the fall of France, in a storm of panic whipped up by the Daily Mail, Churchill had ordered the internment of all 'enemy aliens'. A large proportion were Jewish refugees like Richard, category C internees who were deemed to be of low threat. Questions were asked in the House of Lords about why those with clear anti-Nazi credentials were interned alongside Nazi sympathisers or spies, and why such people were being interned at all. It is possible that anti-Semitism in some levels of government may have played a part.

It appears from contemporary accounts that the organisation around this internment exercise was muddled at best. Internees were given one hour's notice, with some sent at random to the wrong place. They then experienced severe overcrowding in the camps, and shortages of bedding, heating and provisions. This must have been horrendously damaging to those already traumatised by the experiences that had led to their refugee status, and there were several suicides.

Once settled, the internees survived their imprisonment with self-organised programmes of education, music and the arts. I wish I knew more about Richard's experience of his internment at Noverton Avenue in Prestbury. He would have been a valuable member of the cultural circle, with his wide and deep knowledge of modern art and culture. He was probably not the only one to have formerly been a loyal German citizen, even decorated for wartime service some twenty-five years earlier, but who now had to hope their old enemy would defeat their homeland. (In her autobiography, Lilli Palmer describes trying to explain to her English husband, Rex Harrison, why she ardently wishes the allied forces would bomb German cities, to his complete incomprehension.) I imagine Richard's fears, having managed to avoid the Nazi concentration camps, at being taken up now. He was fifty-eight years old, in a country where he only imperfectly spoke the language, and where he had had to leave his defenceless wife and children in another city.

Edith heard that Unwin had helped some refugee publishers with their release from internment; she felt encouraged to ask for help for her husband, too, as he was the past owner of *Delphin-Verlag München*.

Stanley Unwin had taken on the publishing firm of George Allan in 1914, just three years after my grandfather had established *Delphin-Verlag, Landauer u. Zutt* in Munich. By 1934, Unwin was in sole charge of the publishing company George Allen and Unwin Ltd. and remained so until his death in 1968.

However, he held out little hope in his answer to Edith's first letter requesting his support:

> I think it is very doubtful whether I could be of any help in securing the release of your husband from internment. In practice I have found it impossible to achieve anything unless the internee happens to come within one of the categories mentioned in the Government White Paper.

Fortunately, Edith's competence matched her social skills. She replied:

> I quite understand that you can only help me if there is any foundation for an application. My foundation is based on article 19 of the extension of the White Paper.

She explained that, from 1928 to 1932, Richard had been a governing director of *Hirth Verlag München* that published *Die Jugend*. This famous periodical fought against Nazism with words and in cartoons and pictures. Edith visited the library of the British Museum and noted those issues that demonstrated her husband's opinion and activity against Naziism.

> I know it means asking for very much to engage your time and sympathy and I would not have troubled you with this letter, had you not been recommended to me for your kindness and helpfulness.

A further stumbling stone then appeared as his secretary reported that Unwin had had to evacuate his home because of three time bombs, so that 'his movements are at the moment uncertain.' Edith's warm heart made her forget her family's problems to express her concern for his predicament – how like her mother, Cilly!

> I am extremely sorry to hear of your misfortune. I hope you will soon be able to return to your home and find it in the same state you left it.

This was from the woman whose family had lost so much already – home, livelihood, homeland.

Edith's dolphin Christmas card

Stanley Unwin sent the required letter to the Home Office, then all they could do was wait. Months passed. Edith sent Unwin a beautiful, hand-drawn, handwritten Christmas card, showing a dolphin with a small trumpet-blowing cherub. This must have served as a delicate allusion to the relationship between the owner of *Delphin-Verlag* and Unwin.

When Unwin expressed his gratitude and enquired about progress with their application, Edith thanked him but had no good news:

> ... unfortunately, my husband has not yet been released. I got the answer from the Home Office on December 4 that 'the matter is under consideration'. Since then, I heard nothing. I am convinced that he will be released, but it

needs a terribly long time and heaps of patience. Now I hope his release is not very far off.

I could see where my father's optimistic outlook came from.

A long six months after Edith made the first approach to Stanley Unwin, Richard at last won his appeal, but still could not leave internment for another two months. Unwin had interviewed Richard and somewhat apologetically offered him a menial position:

> ...if you are prepared to come here and do junior clerical work, both in our accounts department and in the department that deals with authors' agreements and payments of royalties ... we are prepared to pay £3/10/- a week.

This sum equates to about £250 in today's terms. Status and remuneration were a shadow of Richard's former position as owner of a successful publishing company, but this was nevertheless a great kindness on the part of Stanley Unwin. Further hurdles had to be cleared. Allen and Unwin had to make a declaration that they were unable to fill the position with a native British worker before Richard obtained a work permit. At last, he was free, and could return to their new home in Fitzroy Square.

In the event, Richard was able to oblige with more than administrative duties; the Unwin archive held by Reading University lists several reader's reports written by Richard. Some are on books written in German, on which he was uniquely well-placed to comment. Some were about Germans: *Beethoven*, 1947, by Maria E. Belpaire, and, caustically, *Why Germans are Barbarians*, 1941, by Eleonora Tennant. This last title was somewhat ironic, given *Delphin-Verlag*'s popular First World War series on the topic of *Why Our Enemies* [the British] *Hate Us* [the Germans].

My grandfather's case is described in the book *Britische Buchverlage im internationalen Spannungsfeld 1933–1939* (British Publishers in International Conflict 1933–1939):

> On account of Landauer's fate, but also thanks to the ability of Edith Landauer to provide objective evidence and to strike the right tone of unsentimental honesty, Stanley Unwin also helped in this case, even though Landauer was not known to him as the other emigrants had been.

In my view, it was also her determination, warmth and concern for others that shone through this correspondence and persuaded Unwin to exert himself on Richard's behalf.

In some strange way, my personal search for my own roots is connecting me with others who are on their own journeys of discovery. This network is created through the world wide web, the internet. It is interesting to feel its probing tentacles linking me to other searchers. It is like the invisible underground filament of a fungus; these extensive networks lie out of sight but at random moments offer to one's eye a fruiting body, a mushroom, above the ground.

First, I am contacted by a Herr Jakob, who has come across my blog entry 'Looking for Landauer Roots'. During our six-month house swap to Switzerland, we had started blogging regularly about our experiences (*swissorkney2014*). He wonders what I might know of Richard Adolf Zutt, a Swiss citizen born in 1887 who had died mysteriously on a luxury cruiser 'Gneisenau' in Suez in 1938. Together, we establish that Richard Zutt was not my grandfather's business partner, as Herr Jakob had supposed, but an older brother of Ernst Theodor Zutt. Ernst and my grandfather had owned *Delphin-Verlag* together at its launch in 1911. On the eve of the First World War, Ernst Zutt had left Germany for his native Switzerland, leaving Richard Landauer as sole proprietor of *Delphin-Verlag*.

Another interesting contact comes from Dierk Hoffman, a professor of German at Colgate University, New York. His specialism is literature and culture at the turn of the 20th century, and he asks me about a copy of a novel published by *Delphin-Verlag* in 1914:

> I found in the Yale Library a copy of *Severins Gang in die Finsternis: ein Prager Gepensterroman* (Severin's Walk in the Darkness: a Prague Ghost Story) that confuses me very much: the book has a hard cover and then a soft cover and then the traditional pages. Do any of the books you have from your grandfather have a similar arrangement: that is, have two covers?

Following my trip to the Warburg Institute, I can inform him that several of the *Delphin-Verlag* books have indeed the same arrangement of a double front cover. There is a welcome outcome to our cordial correspondence; he requests the publisher *Vitalis Verlag Prag* to send me a copy of *Severins Gang in die Finsternis: ein Prager Gepensterroman* (2019 Paul Leppin) when they reissue it. To my delight, this contains a facsimile copy of the cover and opening pages from the 1914 *Delphin-Verlag* first edition.

The subjects of the novel are sexuality and the differences between men and women in this regard. Severin, the main character, takes and abandons various lovers until he, in turn, is seduced and then cast off by a woman who understands all his latent sexual urges. Freud's principal work, *The Interpretation of Dreams*, was published in 1900. The nature of female sexuality was of great interest around the turn of the century, with women often depicted either as virginal by nature or else as corrupting whores. The International Psychoanalytic Association was founded ten years later, based on Freud's theories of the power of the unconscious sex drive. Leppin, the author of *Severins Gang in die Finsternis: ein Prager Gepensterroman*, was born in Prague in 1878 and died in 1945 of syphilis and a stroke. My grandfather had not shied from publishing controversial contemporary fiction, I was proud to note.

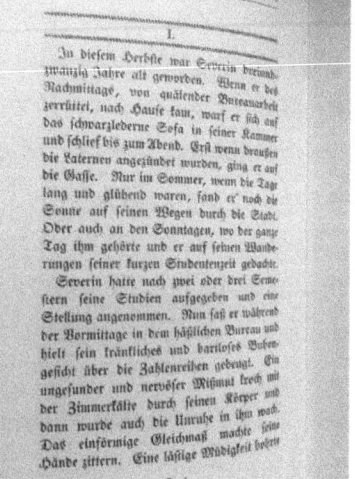

Facsimile of opening pages of Severins Gang in die Finsternis: ein Prager Gepensterroman Severin's Walk in the Darkness: a Prague Ghost Story), first edition, Delphin-Verlag 1914

Delphin-Verlag was Richard's life work, interrupted by two world wars and then taken from him in a long-drawn-out act of legalised theft.

I too have always loved books. I don't remember this but according to my mother, when I was three, I was frequently asked to read from the Times newspaper to impress prospective parents at Mrs Epsom's nursery school in Nairobi. (Mrs Epsom also taught me simple arithmetical operations using bundles of matchsticks, held together in tens by a rubber band – I have always loved mathematics too.) The very first book I could read by myself was a story about a child who thought their stomach rumbling was a homunculus telephoning to say they needed feeding; I was entranced. Books have been my answer to every longueur or grief – when our family dog died, my mother gave me a Marmite sandwich and sent me off to read. I read when I was supposed to be getting up, or going to bed, or tidying my room. I was always so absorbed that I didn't hear my name being called or a parent's footsteps approaching. Then a little later, my parents bought Nipper for me – a bad-tempered elderly beast who had pulled a cart around Derby before being inappropriately repurposed as a child's pony. Their aim was to get me outside and to stop me reading quite so much. My first degree was English literature, necessitating long hours of reading. In my digs, where hot water was free, but heating wasn't, I discovered that reading in the bath or shower was the only way to keep both warm and awake.

My grandfather must have been another such lifelong reader, and ripples from his passion continue to spread.

24

STOLPERSTEINE; LANDSHUT, 2016

From time to time over the years, we children discussed what memorial would be fitting for our father – a bench for walkers near Tissington in the Derbyshire dales? Some sort of plaque in Fitzroy Square, his first home in England? We planted a tree for our mother after her death in 2000, but were still unsure how to commemorate our father's life. He had died a long fourteen years before her, but our discussions had never come to any conclusion.

Then in 2015, the year following our civic ceremony in Landshut, Konrad Haberberger, the chairperson of the Landshut *Stolpersteine* association, writes to me: five more *Stolpersteine* are to be laid in the city centre for my grandfather and his family – for Dr Richard Landauer, his wife Edith, and their children, Eva Maria, Stefan Klaus and Robert Felix. The artist Gunter Demnig will lay the stumbling stones on 25 May 2016. Would we like to attend? This at last feels like a worthy commemoration for our father, placing him with his grandparents and family. We had lost Robert from life some thirty years before, in July 1986. He had begun to leave us seven years before that, as his memory and personality slowly disintegrated. Robert had met so many stumbling stones in his fifty-nine years and, until his last decade, had met them with forward drive and optimism – 'Whatever may happen, I am full of confidence and that *joie de vivre* you mention, and very happy', as he wrote in 1948. And this time, an even bigger group of our extended family plans to accept the invitation.

The thud of the pneumatic drill interrupts the purposeful journeys of Landshut's citizenry, as they traverse the wide high street in the

Altstadt. Many stop to watch Gunter Demnig as he wrestles with the stone cobbles of *Theaterstrasse*; he is the artist whose *Stolpersteine* (stumbling stones) project memorialises victims of National Socialism. He has placed the five new brass-faced cement blocks onto the street surface, next to those commemorating Adolf and Cäcilie Hirsch, and is now drilling the hole for the new ones. The brass gleams against the grey stone. Children sit in a circle around him as if in a trance, their slight bodies throbbing with the vibrating noise. Demnig has to trim one block at its base before it fits. At last, all five are set in place, flush with the surrounding street surface – the *Stolpersteine* for Richard and Edith in one row, with those for their three children aligned beneath. The artist packs dry cement into the surrounding gaps and pours water over the whole from a small can.

Finally, Gunter kneels to wipe each plaque clean. It looks like a gentle act of respectful homage, in sharp contrast to the brutish noise and muscular effort of earlier. The text stands out clearly from each shining brass face:

HIER WOHNTE DR RICHARD LANDAUER JG.1882 FLUCHT 1938 ENGLAND

HIER WOHNTE EDITH LANDAUER GEB. HIRSCH JG.1900 FLUCHT 1938 ENGLAND

HIER WOHNTE EVA MARIA LANDAUER JG.1922 FLUCHT 1938 ENGLAND

HIER WOHNTE STEFAN KLAUS LANDAUER JG.1925 FLUCHT 1938 ENGLAND

HIER WOHNTE ROBERT FELIX LANDAUER JG.1927 FLUCHT 1938 ENGLAND

(Here lived Robert Felix Landauer born 1927 fled 1938 England)

Gunther Demnig

As on our last visit to Landshut, women offer flowers from their baskets to the waiting crowd, and one by one people come forward to lay their offering, a single rose, around the new *Stolpersteine*. It reminds me of the procedure at a funeral, when mourners step up in turn to throw a flower into the open grave, a communal show of solidarity with those grieving a loved one.

Landauer Stolpersteine

As well as the extended Landor family and our partners, the crowd is made up of local people – councillors, Thomas Gambke MdB, Konrad Haberberger and Franz Gervasoni from the Landshut *Stolpersteine Verein*, and many anonymous members of the public. Our German friends are here too – Hans, whose generous efforts had propelled me to this day, and Johanna and her family. This civic ceremony, freely joined by so many Landshut citizens, feels like a fitting memorial for our father, Robert Felix Landauer, who had been a part of the Landshut community for the last period of his German childhood.

The *Stolpersteine* ceremony is followed by a reception, where an exhausted Gunter Demnig addresses us. He explains that the trigger for the *Stolpersteine* project was the assertion by an inhabitant of an apartment block he visited that no Romany had ever lived there. Gunter knew as a fact that some had – he knew their names and their stories. They had fled or been ejected from their homes when the National Socialists came to power, never to return. It came to him then that these people, and millions like them, had been removed from local memory as well as from life. He had the idea of creating these 'stumbling stones', so that passers-by would have a jolt to consciousness, a prompt to remember those who had once been an integral part of their community.

The mood lightens as Gunter describes one occasion when he had looked up from his completion of a *Stolperstein* installation to see two groups of people staring at each other in shock. They had each been unaware of the existence of their father's secret other family. We express our grateful appreciation to him, over sandwiches and cakes provided by the community, and glasses of Orkney Highland Park malt whisky that we took with us for this occasion.

The day begins with an invitation to our young people to meet with Green Party MP Thomas Gambke MdB, to discuss our international relationships. It ends with a typical Bavarian meal in a restaurant, hosted by our kind friends, Johanna's parents. As we eat *wurst* and drink *bier*, I reflect that the treat of a meal in a restaurant may have been part of Robert's Landshut experience too.

Johanna is taking a warm interest in our visit to instal *Stolpersteine* for my father and his family. She was one of the original *Stolpersteine* project students, and subsequently visited us in Scotland. We are staying with her family on this second visit to Landshut. She and her father, Wolfgang, have generously taken it upon themselves to interpret between our two languages and cultures. Johanna takes us around an exhibition commemorating the student resistance group, the White Rose, whom the Nazis arrested and executed; as a student now at the same university, the University of Munich, she feels a strong interest in these martyrs. Her mother, Bernadette, ensures we are well fed with bountiful local specialities – dumplings, casseroles, shredded pancakes – and we want for nothing. Their English is faultless and yet again I determine to try harder to learn German. They regale us with their favourite English-language songs and shows, astounded that we have never seen Freddy Frinton's Dinner for One sketch, with his brilliant performance as the drunk butler. Many Germans, they assure us, watch it every New Year, and now we do too.

Our family party agree to meet the day after the *Stolpersteine* ceremony, so that I can show Villa Hirsch to those who weren't with us on the previous visit. Again, we wander along *Brühfeldweg*, admiring the luxurious properties on each side of the road, and again we stop in the driveway of Villa Hirsch, looking up at the imposing façade, and discussing how it differs from the original. This time, however, it turns out we are not alone. An upstairs window shoots open, and a woman's head appears, querying sharply what this large gawping party was doing on her property. Luckily, Johanna has accompanied us on the trip, and she steps forward to explain in German who we are and why we have come. We stand waiting through this exchange, shifting awkwardly from foot to foot, embarrassed by having been caught trespassing. Johanna's lengthy explanation has a calming effect, and the acerbity leaves the owner's voice.

Finally Johanna turns to us.

'This lady lives in the apartment where your great-grandparents lived – she knows their story. She apologises that she cannot invite you in today but asks if you would all come to see her at 11 a.m. tomorrow.'

Of course, we are delighted to accept, although still feeling mortified by our temerity, and numerousness. The next day, we ring the doorbell and introduce ourselves to Angelika and her second husband, Manfred. Angelika first shows us round the apartment. Much of it showcases the work of her late first husband, a well-known artist of stained-glass windows. Angelika herself is a gifted painter, and we see some of her work too. In every corridor and room there are paintings, prints and art objects, such that I want to linger for hours. But she ushers us into a room whose balcony has been converted into an upstairs conservatory. Seated around a large table, our hosts ply us with buttered pretzels, beer, and soft drinks. Angelika shows us photos of Manfred on horseback; he takes part in every cycle of the Landshut wedding pageant and looks very dashing.

As we begin to take our leave, expressing our heartfelt thanks for their hospitality, Angelika draws me to one side. She shows me a framed photo of Cilly that she keeps on a special shelf. At the laying of the *Stolpersteine* for the Hirsches in 2013, she had learnt for the first time how Cilly had met her death. The conservatory where we had just been sitting was the balcony from which Cilly had fallen, she tells me. Since this discovery she has lit a candle for Cilly, next to this photo, on each anniversary of her birth and of her death. I feel a strong connection to this kind, warm woman – very like Cilly herself, I think – and we hug.

Manfred takes us through the apartment as he escorts us downstairs to the outside door. The villa must have been converted back to residential use, extended and divided into flats, since its days as a sanatorium when my parents had visited it in 1969. We are shown the perfectly kept quadrangle of garages and outbuildings, where they have turned one of the original small cottages into a painting studio for Angelika. Then we are taken through the belt of trees to see the summer house I had set my heart on at my last visit. Its main feature is the lead roof, which is curved and wrapped over the walls, creating a shapely bonnet. Unlike the severe lines of the original Villa Hirsch, its shape looks whimsical; fairy-tale creatures might emerge from the door or peep through the windows. If only I could buy it ... I imagine myself there, camping and cooking outdoors in the summer, and lighting a small iron stove in the winter while I hibernate, writing – a secret home for a Landauer, with Cilly's spirit watching over me.

25

TWO HALVES; REFLECTION

I open the email with eager anticipation. My second cousin, the son of Margaret's cousin, Pamela, recently signed up with a genetic ancestry company and sent off his saliva sample. He phoned me:

'One surprise: there's a small percentage of Swedish DNA in my sample! Mum has no idea how that got there ... Some blond Viking, or a Swedish au pair from the past, do you think?'

'Who knows? But if I get my DNA tested too, I could see if there's any Swedish in mine. That should show whether it's from our side of the family or your dad's ... '

I searched online for a good deal on DNA investigation and submitted my sample. Here at last are the results, after some weeks of waiting.

I am 49.8% Ashkenazi Jew. For some reason this surprises me, though I can't think why it should. It also gives me something solid to grasp hold of, after my childhood as an expat trying to fit in to so many new cultures. This is the racial element of who I am: 45.7% British and Irish, 4.3% French and German, and almost 50% Jewish (but no Swedish). By adopting the Christian religion of the majority among whom they lived, perhaps my Jewish ancestors felt they would be safer – although to be sure, genocides occur along religious lines. But you can choose your religion, whether to hide or to display it, whether to change to another or to have none. You cannot choose your race.

Nevertheless, in the case of Jewish people, they can often hide their race; the Jewish stereotype of dark curly hair, dark eyes, swarthy skin and a large nose is not so different from other South European types as to be instantly recognisable. Indeed, the Nazis insisted Jews wear a yellow star to ensure they were identifiable, and many Jews survived the war living 'underground', hiding among the general population. My father had dark, wavy hair and dark brown eyes. My brother has mid-brown, straight hair and lighter brown eyes. My sister and I have fair, brown hair and blue eyes. I don't think you could tell by looking that any of us, father or children, are Jewish by race.

Our modern Western consciousness tends to slide over the concept of race, so as to be inclusive and non-discriminatory. We are trying to separate ourselves from the racist attitudes and crimes committed by our colonising ancestors. And yet to the DNA scientists in the genetic ancestry company, race is a factual, measurable differential. It is our response to it we should scrutinise. David Baddiel complains in *Jews Don't Count* that anti-Semitism is deemed a less important racism than other forms, for example against people of colour. In Britain today, Jews are marginal but not marginalised, he argues, almost white and therefore privileged, connected in the public mind with wealthy, powerful dynasties such as Rothschild and Warburg. They thus are deemed to deserve no pity. Yet in his comedy sketches, he is explicitly racist, blacking up and stereotyping, which has the effect of destroying sympathy for his argument against antisemitism.

Popular consciousness also links Jews with the Zionist state of Israel and its genocidal treatment of Palestine. In media culture in the US, the stereotypical Jew is a hapless, neurotic intellectual – think Woody Allen films. Baddiel's Twitter bio consists of one word, Jew; the adjective 'Jew' is often flung as an insult – compare 'Jew banker' to 'Jewish banker' – and he is consciously reclaiming the term. In a similar way, 'quaker' was a derisive description of the behaviour of early Friends Society members, who then took it up proudly, to be known thereafter as Quakers. Delving deeper, there is a growing debate about the divisions within the different branches of Jewish race, with Arab,

Mizrahi and Sephardi Jews decrying the 'transnational Ashkenormative supremacy' of Ashkenazi Jews.

I have to wonder about my own attitude to Jewishness. Why was I always so keen to explain that though my father's family were racially Jewish, causing their enforced flight from Germany, they were not Jewish by religion? My father's cousin, Dora, and her husband, Ted Schocken, practising Jews, invited us to a Friday Sabbath dinner in New York; I found their prayers and customs around food entirely strange. But then, I found them no stranger than the Christian American families we knew in Ghana, who held hands around the table while saying an interminably long grace before eating. I tell people I am half German, meaning the nationality, which is a politically determined and variable dimension, as borders can and do shift. It has never occurred to me to say I am half Jewish, which is my racial identity. Do I have some internalised shame about Jewishness, any anti-Semitism of my own? The phenomenon is not unknown. Anna Freud noted after the war that, to her surprise, some Jewish child refugees identified with Nazis, perhaps to gain some feeling of control in their extreme powerlessness. This identification with an aggressor has since been noted in other minority groups. One might claim that to assimilate into a non-Jewish culture – as my grandfather, Richard, and his family did when they adopted the mainstream Catholic faith of Bavarian Germany – implies a rejection of Jewishness. Perhaps I inherited this attitude, at a deeply subconscious level.

When Robert wrote the long letter to his brother about their difficult relationships with Richard, he was lying in a tent on a fruit farm in Kent, following his demobilisation from national service. He explained that the day's work had been abandoned because it was raining, as they could not pick cherries during or after rain.

He didn't complain about the loss of wages, or being cold or stuck indoors. He made the best of it, as always:

> I am writing on my straw bed, propped up against my rucksack, with ground sheets over and under me, and my blanket over my shoulders. And it's not at all a bad home, this large ex-army tent, about 12' by 12', x 6' high, and quite waterproof, and I am really quite comfortable in it.

This Pollyannaism is despite his later admission that the tent overheated and was unbearably stuffy in the warm summer weather. They could not leave the tent door open, he said, for fear of thieving hens, wildlife and men.

He had used his day of enforced leisure to reflect on his family and to communicate his thoughts and feelings. As I write about my own exploration of identity and belonging, chance occurrences in the present day are similarly deepening my opportunities for reflection. One such example is my recent viewing of Tom Stoppard's play, *Leopoldstadt*. Ever since Ted Schocken took us to see *Rosencrantz and Guildenstern Are Dead* in New York over fifty years ago, I have loved Stoppard's intelligence and wit. I take any opportunity to see a new play of his. How strange then that his latest, *Leopoldstadt*, explores so many of the same issues that I am grappling with. What does it mean to be Jewish? To convert to Christianity, or to marry a non-Jew? To be successfully assimilated into a predominantly non-Jewish culture, rather than living in a ghetto among fellow Jews? The extended Merz family, his main characters, might almost have been the Landauers, with their roots in textile manufacturing. Both families made marriages to non-Jews, and had art and music and literature at the heart of their aesthetic lives; both experienced the destruction of their lives following *Anschluss*, with many of them meeting tragic ends.

In the opening scene, Christmas 1899, Grandma Emilia Merz is writing captions in a family photo album, using white ink on the matt black pages; my English mother did the same with the Landauer family photos. I think Margaret would have agreed with Emilia's assertion that losing your name in a family album is 'like a second death'. At first everyone knows who each face belongs to but, as time passes, fewer and fewer people recognise them. In the Landauer family album that my mother tried to annotate after my father's death, she could only label many pages with an approximate year. While I can identify the immediate family members, most others are unknown to me. It is already too late for these Landauers to be held in memory.

One of the play's characters asserts that to be assimilated does not mean to stop being Jewish, but rather to remain Jewish 'without insult', without that being a problem, as was the case for other minority religions or sects in Vienna. That was surely the Landauer experience in Munich in the 1920s; they were Germans, fully assimilated, part of the Christian mainstream, and were doing well. Like Hermann Merz, the Landauer family used their growing wealth to engage in fine art and culture. Richard was perhaps slow to understand the full implications of the Nazi extremism of the early 1930s; he wrote that some of his published series must be acceptable in the new regime because they celebrated German culture. When did he stop thinking of himself as a loyal German – or did he ever?

The Theresienstadt ghetto, where my great-grandfather Adolf Hirsch lost his life through starvation, illness or violence, was also the final destination for some of Stoppard's characters. One of the Merz family, Leo, has been brought up as an English boy, after his widowed mother married an Englishman. He says he feels fortunate to belong to this 'top country'. My father and his siblings were determinedly English too. Leo tells us he didn't know he had an accent until he lost it, unlike my father who never did lose his, apparently. (I am reminded of that old quip: how can you tell which ones are refugees? Those are the ones who have lost everything except their accents.) Leo also says he was pleased to have Jewish blood – he sees it as an 'exotic fact' about himself. That seems to be how my mother viewed my father's background.

The audience is told that, at that time, fifty per cent of university graduates, professional and creative people were Jewish, despite Jews making up only ten percent of Vienna's population. There was a pride in being Jewish and cultured; I can see glimpses of this when Robert refers to 'that great Jew Victor Gollancz', and when Stephen writes to Dr Schier that Richard was 'the first to publish Picasso'.

Stoppard only discovered the full story of his Jewish family in the 1990s, and *Leopoldstadt* draws heavily on his findings. Some twenty years later, I am following a similar journey. I too feel the need to transmit the knowledge that I am uncovering, before it is lost to the generations to come.

Just after the Second World War, charitable organisations in England looked after orphans rescued from concentration camps. The rhetoric around these child survivors was that, with sufficient resources and care, the children could recover from their harrowing start in life. This must have been the belief Edith subscribed to when she went to work in the Anna Freud kindergarten for refugee children. The message that children can be helped to recover from trauma had to be drummed in as the organisers needed funding: give now to help these innocent children return to normal health and happiness.

Increasingly, however, we learn that trauma is not so easily set aside. My aunt's mental illness, my uncle's refusal to let his children know anything about their family history – perhaps even my father's early-onset dementia? – may all have had their roots in the dispossession and abuse they experienced in their childhood and while they were developing into adults. After all, adolescence, like toddlerhood, is a critical time of rapid change and vulnerability, when the plasticity of the brain means that adverse childhood experiences can have a tremendous impact. Eva, Stefan and Robert ranged in age from six to sixteen during those grim years from 1933 to 1938.

Recent research shows that trauma gives rise to epigenetic change, altering the chemistry of a person's DNA. This happens when a brain is repeatedly flooded with cortisol, the stress hormone that triggers the fight, flight or freeze survival mechanism. Subsequent generations can therefore inherit trauma, and response to trauma, from grandparents and parents, through their genes. Both my parents lived through a war, and their parents before them had survived the First World War.

A socially constructed learnt behaviour may be added on top of biological change. We may continue the coping mechanism used by a parent, even if it's a dysfunctional one, because that was our model during childhood. We are formed by our family, through our inheritance of values and culture, identity and relationship patterns, as well as through our genetic makeup. This can stretch backwards a long way.

And of course, each sibling responds differently; they are affected by their position in the family, by an event's critical timing in their different trajectories of development, by their personalities and genetic makeup, and by the protective factors available to each one (which may or may not include each other).

There were severe adverse events in my father's early life, but perhaps he also had stronger protective forces than my mother. Margaret had no siblings. Robert had been very close to his brother, as seen from his letters, and both his mother and his grandmother were exceptionally warm, nurturing women. Certainly, he was not interested in conforming to society's expectations, instead enjoying the company of like-minded people, irrespective of their race or social position in life, whereas my mother cared a little more about fitting in with the right set of people. Perhaps this was more important half a century ago, in a small market town like Ashbourne where Margaret grew up and where everyone knew each other's background and their place in the social structure. She had returned to her hometown to build a family home, to give us some stability.

I had felt a sense of security once I settled into Ashbourne's Queen Elizabeth Grammar School. It makes me wonder why, despite the fact that QEGS had a boarding house, I was sent away to boarding school in York after only two terms at QEGS, when Robert took a post in Guyana. If I had stayed on there I would have been in the same town as my grandparents, Fred and Mabel Kirkland. Did my mother think I would be held back by this environment? Since my brother was already at boarding school and seemed happy enough, she may have thought I would benefit from being in the same city as him, though it transpired we were only allowed to meet for an hour once a term on Sunday exeats. In addition, Margaret had been brought up in a time and place of highly stratified social classes and had, through education and through marriage, transferred herself to a different social class, as indeed had been her mother, Mabel's, ambition for her. She may have been anxious not to lose this advancement, as she saw it, for the next generation. We now believe that secure attachment relationships are more important, but each generation acts according to the culture of their time. Margaret embraced with courage all the opportunities her new life offered, but nevertheless she coped poorly with stress. This can be a sign of imposter syndrome. Perhaps she had the same stumbling stone as I did, a fear of not belonging.

From research we know trauma can result in insecure attachment and in negative coping mechanisms such as perfectionism, a need for control, or a dependence on alcohol or drugs. Early experience of abandonment or loss can lead to an off-the-scale response to the slightest trigger, to hypervigilance and to catastrophising when minor things go wrong. A seemingly adapted child may be too ready to please and meet others' wishes, and be unaware of their own needs. This is just as true of the embodied trauma that is inherited through the genes, with its invisible roots. Although I have only recently learnt about my father's family's repeated loss and trauma, I can see this inheritance in some of my behaviours. For example, it explains my inability to handle suspense; I tend to choose a less good option rather than waiting to see if a better one transpires. In other words, anxiety makes maintaining a sense of control more important for me than the uncertainty of keeping options open in hope. My mother's determination to keep on working through my father's last years, because of an excessive fear for her financial future, was a similar symptom of anxiety, and was perhaps inherited from her parents. So this stumbling stone, of dysfunctional response to stress, may be threefold: one layer inherited through my genes, one imitated through a model and one triggered by my own fragmented childhood.

I am reminded of a bilingual family where the German mother always spoke in German to her children, while her Scottish husband always spoke in English, thus providing the distinct language communities a child needs when learning to communicate in two tongues. This worked well with their first two children, and their daughters grew up fluent in both German and English, switching seamlessly between them. However, their next child, a boy, refused ever to speak German even though it was clear he could understand it. They concluded that he was following a gendered model: men and boys speak English, and women and girls speak German. I wish I had modelled myself on my even-tempered father but instead I seem to have followed the example of my mother in her reaction to stress. Daughters learn from what their mothers do, rather than from what they say.

I'm finding, though, that the very act of exploring and understanding the roots of my reaction is helping me to overcome it. Sifting through the layers of historical and current emotional responses in my family and in myself means I can begin to process them, and not hand them down unthinkingly to the next generations. Ruptures are inevitable in any interaction; what is critical is how one repairs them.

The Loganair plane takes off from Kirkwall airport, and banks over Orkney's white sandy bays and turquoise sea. I reclaim my attention from the view and listen once more to the familiar safety announcement: '... guide you to your nearest exit, bearing in mind that it may be behind you.' This is what I have been doing in writing this book – finding my way out of confusion by repairing the rent in the fabric of my life. I am beginning to put it behind me.

26

FITZROY SQUARE; LONDON, 2017

My brother and I visit Fitzroy Square, where the Landauer family first lived in those post-war years, on a dry autumn day. The trees in the centre are changing colour, setting off the elegant beauty of the four-storey Georgian square, which is now mostly pedestrianised. The house we are looking for is on the west side, built later than the Adams-designed east side but in faithful imitation of it. We stand on the pavement, admiring the wrought-iron balcony, the curved stonework over the windows and front door fanlight, the high drawing-room windows, the verdant window boxes. I think about the flat where Robert had grown up in *Elisabethstrasse* in Munich. This gracious building has a similar feel to it.

As we peer towards the door, trying to work out whether the building is single or multiple occupancy, the sash window on the ground floor flies up.

'Can I help you?' is spoken in steely tones, accompanied by a volley of defensive barking from behind her.

'Sorry to bother you – we just found out our father lived in this house with his family in the late 1930s, early 1940s.'

The owner and her small dog have their alarm allayed by our explanation. Although she still doesn't invite us in, she gives us the history of the building, as far as she knows it. Before her ownership, the house belonged to a small art charity, but there the trail grew cold. I have to rely on my imagination to people this beautiful abode with the Landauers.

I think about their Christmases in this new place. They arrived in September 1938, so they were able to celebrate Christmas that year, and

230

the following year too, as far as wartime shortages and bomb damage allowed. If nothing else, they would have had their music, singing and playing the old German carols – '*Stille Nacht, heilige Nacht*' (Silent Night, Holy Night); '*O Tannenbaum, O Tannenbaum, Wie grün sind Deine Blätter*' (Oh Christmas Tree, Oh Christmas Tree, How Green Are Your Leaves). Perhaps they even found some green branches to decorate with coloured cut-outs from scraps of paper and homemade *Lebkuchen* (gingerbread). Christmas 1940 would have been difficult as Richard was separated from them in the internment camp, with no word of when he would be released, but there was hope that it might not be too long. By the Christmas of 1941, it must have seemed that all was finally turning out well for the Landauer family. Richard was not only back home; he was also in employment, working with his beloved books again. The boys were on holiday from boarding school, no doubt relieved to be free from lessons and homework. Edith was helping at Anna Freud's kindergarten for refugee children. She would have been enjoying being with little ones, sharing her warmth and love, helping others who were less fortunate than themselves. They had come through so much; no one could have dreamt that, rather than heralding a new beginning, this would be their last Christmas together as a family.

1942 passed as peacefully as it could for a Jewish family in wartime London. They could at last establish routines – work, school, running the household. As December approached, they would have begun preparations for their next Christmas, their fifth in London, but then tragedy struck.

Edith, whose charm and skills had secured Richard's release from internment; Edith, on whose warm common sense so many relied; the grandmother I never knew – Edith succumbed rapidly to a massive infection. Perhaps it was salmonella, perhaps influenza. She probably picked it up in the Anna Freud kindergarten where she volunteered. She died just a few days before Christmas.

Like her mother Cilly, Edith had a generous nature, a quick empathy and a warm integrity that won people to her. It was these characteristics that had helped her husband out of internment and into the dignity of employment. And now she was gone.

On December 20, 1947, Robert wrote to his father:

> Yesterday it was five years since Mother died, and even more than usual, all our thoughts were centred on her who was always joyful and happy, who had such abundant love and faith ... I always hope that you might also find that inward peace that Mother had in such great measure – that inner tranquillity that is born out of sure faith and love, that does not permit us to worry over little or big things – that allowed Mother to be gay and cheerful, to be happy and to enjoy life even in the face of terrible odds, and that makes her monument stand not in Marylebone Cemetery, but in our hearts and lives.

I could feel the immense weight of this tragedy – she was the warm, beating heart at their centre. There are no words sufficient to imagine the impact of her sudden death, which was in any case unique to each family member. How could Richard survive another loss, coming on top of so much else? Would Eva have to look after him now, instead of establishing herself in independent adult life? Stephen, the serious, sensitive one of the family, no longer had his mother to protect him. And my father, Robert Felix *Floh*, the happy flea, was just fifteen years of age, so young to be without a mother. Edith could never be forgotten by those who loved her. I was born a decade after her death, but despite never having met her, I feel I know her through these testimonies.

The children had also lost their grandmother, Cilly, only a year earlier, although the news of her death had probably not yet reached them. Grandmothers mostly fare well in literature. They can often stand in for a mother, offering home and love and comfort in her place. They transmit the family culture, their language, food and customs. Tove Jansson's *Summer Book* describes a child's experience of living with her redoubtable, all-seeing grandmother on a small island, helping her forage and keep house:

> 'Do you believe I can dive without me showing you?' the child asked.

> 'Yes, of course,' Grandmother said ... she thought, 'I must remember to tell [the child's father] this child is still afraid of deep water.'

And in children's literature, wee Katie Morag gets into trouble delivering the mail when her family's problems of trying to manage the shop with a teething baby get too much. Her 'Granny Island' rescues her and puts everything right, giving her a ride home on the islanders' ubiquitous grey Fergie tractor.

I have recently become a grandmother, and I know at first hand the close bond that exists in this relationship. Grandmothers have a double thread binding them to the nurture of their grandchildren. We feel a strong, quasi-maternal love as we search for reminders of our own lineage in the genetic mélange that produced this child. We relive those precious 'happy family' memories of the time when our own children were little. I'm remembering with pride, for example, that my daughter, aged two, became completely independent using a hammer and nails at the woodwork bench as she accompanied me to the playgroup I ran. My little granddaughter assured my daughter that 'Nana will sew you a new dress just like the one Nana made for me'. This grandchild is our own flesh and blood, and we revel in new achievements and examples of cuteness and cleverness. In addition, that child's parent is our own child, who, even as an adult, still holds our unconditional love and protectiveness.

As I write this, sitting on a park bench in the sunshine, a grandmother has just walked past me, hand in hand with a little girl.

'I've got carrot soup for you, and I've got rolls as well!' she promises. The love and trust in their relationship is so clear to see and I can't help smiling as they pass.

Edith and I were born into different worlds, different cultures and different languages, but I feel certain that we would have had this close relationship. Her untimely death was an important loss for me too, the granddaughter who could never know her. I make a promise to myself: I will be an active and present grandmother, mother, wife, sister, aunt. And I will take on from my mother the mantel of story keeper for my father's family.

27

ROBERT'S SLOW DECLINE; REFLECTION

Several years after Robert died, aged only fifty-nine, our mother was sent the results of his brain autopsy. We didn't know why it had taken so long, and had almost forgotten one was being done. By the time of his death in 1986, the ugly term 'premature senility' – so distressing when applied to our outgoing, sociable dad who had been *Floh* and Felix in childhood – had given way to a more specific diagnosis, Alzheimer's disease. This disorder was gaining greater awareness in the public mind around this time; November 1983 was declared the first National Alzheimer's Month. We knew only a little in those days: that aluminium was involved, so we threw away a lot of saucepans, and that it could be inherited, but this warning we ignored, having already started our family.

The autopsy results were startling; Robert had not had Alzheimer's. There were no signs of the typical cauliflower growths or lesions in his brain. So, we asked, what had caused the dementia? They could not tell us. It might have been a knock on the head (he had banged his head when he slipped whilst moving a stone sundial, we remembered), or it could have been caused by a virus ... A virus? Surely that just causes colds, we thought. Then we remembered the bat.

When our family lived in Guyana, we and some friends had taken a trip into the interior to see the Kaieteur Falls, the highest vertical waterfall in the world. We were given an army escort, partly because it was dangerous and partly as an exercise for the troops, and we travelled in a caravan of bone-shaking jeeps. For the last section of the journey,

Amerindians took us upriver in dugout canoes, looking around warily for anacondas, electric eels and piranha fish. We were told about a recent death in that area, when a man had stepped on an electric eel hidden in water made murky by vegetation. At last we reached the top of the Falls, and we teenagers stepped tentatively into the Pepsicola-coloured waters. We stayed a safe distance away from the thundering edge. Even at an inch deep, we could feel the dangerous tug of the current.

The nearby rest-house had been double-booked by a party on its way down from the Falls, so we camped at night. We women were in a stuffy tent (which I bitterly resented) while the men had mattresses under a tarpaulin to keep the dew and tree-drips off them. Before we turned in, we sat entranced by the flickering sheet lightning, which momentarily erased all the constellations of the southern hemisphere, the Milky Way and the shooting stars.

It rained overnight, and the tarpaulin over the men's hammocks filled up. It had been punctured in a few places to prevent it collapsing under the weight of water. Later that night, Robert awoke and felt his feet were wet. Assuming that some part of the awning had failed, but not too disastrously, he went back to sleep. When daylight came, we were shocked to find that his sleeping bag was soaked in blood. A vampire bat had crept down his body to find his toe, and had bitten him, injecting him with its anticoagulant saliva to keep the blood flowing.

It made a good story to dine out on, part of our family's mad adventures. But perhaps that was when he was infected with a virus. My mother-in-law, Nancy, who had been a colleague of Robert's at Swansea University in the 1970s, told me that she thought he had showed signs of the developing dementia long before it caused his first collapse in 1979.

I like to think that if this were to happen in our family now, this dementia diagnosis for a loved one, we would manage the seven years between diagnosis and death so much better. There are local and national support systems, and lots of accessible information. But that was not how it was then. I think Margaret was terrified of having to support everyone by herself. Her husband was losing all capacity, and her parents were still alive and in their late eighties. We children were in those stages of late childhood and early adulthood where we had our own crucial commitments – to finish education, establish a career, bring up small children, and so on. None of us lived in Ashbourne; we were spread between Essex, Orkney and London. And, as I now remember from that illness she had when we were at boarding school, she was incapable of asking for help.

In fact, she just seemed furious all the time, and would snap at me when I tried to enquire about our father, or how she was coping. I walked on eggshells around her, feeling useless, and cried after bruising visits or phone calls. On top of this heavy guilt, of feeling powerless to help, there was the permanent worry about his safety, as our mother continued to teach full-time. She was consumed by financial anxiety, knowing herself to be the sole carer and provider. So, Robert was left alone all day, to smoke his cigarettes, wander down the road, and eat all the sweet things he could find, but since I was too far away to take up any responsibility myself, I felt I had no right to criticise. It was such a miserable time, even whilst I was revelling in the loveliness of our growing children.

I am remembering an occasion when the whole Landor family had gathered at our parents' home in Ashbourne for an early summer week. That afternoon the weather was kind. We stretched out bare arms and legs, pale in their first exposure of the year, to gather the sun's rays. My sister, Reni, helped our mother carry out trays of beer and juice, crisps and biscuits, while Mark angled his camera lens around our party.

'Mim – say cheese!'

I removed my absorbed gaze from our baby and toddler playing beside me on the picnic rug and smiled up at the camera. A few weeks later, once we were back home in Orkney, he sent me an envelope of photos – a keepsake of that joyous family occasion. One image, though, held me longest: behind the bright group in the centre of the picture is the dark shape of a man trying to escape. My father. He could no longer cope with noise, with social events, but made no fuss; he just crept away. It still breaks my heart to remember.

I have recently re-read Sally Magnusson's *Where Do Memories Go?* and have been musing over the vast variety of ways dementia changes people. Sally's mother, Mamie, maintained her facility with words and wit almost until the end. Another old lady we knew would repeat the same joke punchline every few minutes, trilling with laughter each time. For my father, it was the opposite. He didn't speak, and tried to avoid interaction wherever it occurred. Robert had retreated into anxiety and silent depression, so different from his former outgoing self. None of us knew how to engage with him, how to just be beside him in his locked-in state. This was decades, too, before they understood that familiar music has enormous power to tap into memory. Music had been such a large part of Robert's pleasure in life, as he whistled his way through any chore. How could this be the same man whose easy interest in his fellow humans drew people to him, friends and strangers alike? Where had his gift for connectedness gone? And why? It was the cruellest punishment, for this man who didn't believe in punishment. And we didn't know how to reach him. Robert's only comfort was a young marmalade cat, who had turned up at our house on the axle of a friend's car. As the friend had no idea when the kitten had started its ride, he couldn't return it, and Robert seemed to take to it. We named the cat Felix, in honour of our father, and indeed the pair seemed to bring each other a measure of happiness.

We were so ignorant, and too young. My lifelong preponderance towards an anxious guilt leached into black shame. I felt I was a bad daughter, avoidant, worthless. Guilt, and shame. Is this what all family members of dementia sufferers feel?

In the summer of 1986, Robert developed pneumonia, and it was clear that he was dying. I got a flight from Orkney with our youngest, a baby of a few months, and was in time to see him on his last day. As I sat by his bed, he smiled and reached his hand to stroke his new granddaughter's cheek. For that brief instant, it felt as if my real father had returned. At his funeral, I cried uncontrollably, looking across at his coffin. At last, the sad silent shadow in my recent memory could be replaced by the man I remembered through all my growing up – and now he was gone. The last seven years had felt so confusing; the father, who could have supported me through those early years of marriage, job-finding and childbearing, had disappeared. But until now I couldn't mourn him, as his physical shell was still there, sitting in his favourite armchair with Felix on his knee.

The death of Klaus Barbie five years later made a big impact on me. I had pulled the car over, with great care and into an official layby, because I had slowly become aware that there was a blue flashing light behind me. It was 1991, and I had been returning home from a visit to a client family, while listening transfixed to the news on the car radio.

'You were going it a bit there.'

The police officer standing at my car window heard my garbled apology in silence.

'I know, I *was* going too fast. I'm so sorry. And past a school too. I know speed limits are really important – I have children myself ... '

At length, my self-recriminations ran down. I must have said everything he was planning to say to me, as after a nerve-wracking pause, he angled his thumb along the road and said, 'Get along then.'

The reason my foot had pressed more and more heavily on the accelerator was because of my internal conflict. The death of Klaus Barbie, the 'Butcher of Lyon', imprisoned for Nazi war crimes long after the war had ended, was the main news item. He died of cancer soon after his incarceration, on 25 September 1991, aged 77. At that time, I felt it was wrong to pursue and put on trial old, ill men, for events so long past in history.

My father built his life work on principles of rehabilitation, not on punishment, I remembered. As a probation officer, he tried to help prisoners make the transition back to civilian life, with his trademark optimistic good cheer giving hope to all around him. Later when he worked for UNDP in Guyana, the boys at the approved school were appreciative of his transformative work with them; they shaved their heads in his honour, mimicking his baldness pattern, a bare U surrounding a tuft of hair at the front.

Perhaps I was also thinking of Robert's last years, a sad shrinking man whose memory and capacity to communicate had gradually ebbed away – old and ill long before his time. My imagination flashed up an image of Barbie as a trembling, confused man being led to the courtroom dock, unable to understand what was happening around him, and I felt sick.

And yet as I listened to the radio, there came into my mind the atrocities in Rwanda, in Cambodia, in Bosnia ... Crimes against humanity, genocides, were still being committed all over the world. It came to me that it was crucial for the furtherance of my father's civilised values that justice was pursued, and was seen to be pursued, with no exceptions. Something was beginning to shift in my understanding of the world, and of my family's place in it.

28

REMEMBERING CILLY'S STORY; REFLECTION

'Get her out!'

The wife of the Nazi storm trooper screamed at the orderlies wheeling my great-grandmother's bed into the hospital ward.

'Not in here! I will not share this room with a dirty Jew. I will report you; you will lose your job.'

There was no point in resisting. They pushed the bed back out into the corridor, where, alone and in great pain, Cäcilie Hirsch died the next day, on 30 October 1941.

I never met Cilly, as she died more than a decade before I was born, but she appears several times in *Change Lobsters and Dance*, the autobiography of her niece, Lilli Palmer. Cilly's story taught me that resistance, defined as 'refusal to accept or comply', can take many forms.

To recap, Cäcilie Hirsch, known affectionately to everyone as Cilly and 100% Ashkenazi Jew, was my great-grandmother. Her daughter, Edith, was my father's mother. Cilly was the second of a Berlin doctor's five daughters. She was also a fully assimilated Bavarian *Hausfrau* and mother of three children (two living and one dead).

Cilly had married Adolf Hirsch, another Ashkenazi Jew, who made his fortune by creating Landshut's premier high street department store,

Kaufhaus Tietz Nachfolger. He built Villa Hirsch for his family, that beautiful manor house overlooking the city.

Cilly was Lilli Palmer's favourite aunt, indeed the only one of her mother's four elder sisters that she wrote about. Lilli noted that Cilly was calm and nurturing, looking after everyone else right from the word go. Cilly and Adolf were benefactors for their town community, to the extent that, despite being Jewish, he was made an honorary member of the *Turngemeinde*, a civic society of local worthies who did charitable works from their positions of power.

Unfortunately, according to Lilli, Adolf also took advantage of his position of power by impregnating his young shop assistants. Cilly did not make a show of anger or distress, the typical response of the wronged spouse. Instead, she visited the police to pay the fines, getting Adolf released from prison, and ensuring that his victims were financially supported. The townspeople did their best to protect her from these interviews with authority, because she was so well loved, Lilli wrote. Nowadays we would have many critical questions about both the veracity and the morality of this anecdote, with none of Lilli's complacent chuckles, but her point remains: Cilly resisted adopting the clichéd persona of aggrieved wife and instead took positive action, showing dignity and compassion.

Shortly before war broke out, Cilly visited her elder sister, Rose Peiser, and her nieces Irene, Lilli and Hilde, in London's Parsifal Road, where they were now living, having fled Berlin. The Peisers did their utmost to persuade Cilly to stay with them. I try to imagine what the conversation would have been:

'We can help you get Adolf to Switzerland – we have some funds there. Then he can join you here.'

'Thank you! But no, I have to go back home.'

So they took her to the street to show her the throngs bustling by.

'Look! These people are all free!'

Cilly must have felt tempted to accept, to gain liberty for herself and for her husband, but she resisted their pleading, instead doing what she thought was right.

'You see, every week I try to send a hundred food parcels to people in concentration camps – relatives, friends, sometimes strangers too. One is only permitted to do that from within Germany's borders. So I have to go back. I must send my packages.'

She returned to Adolf and to Landshut.

Lilli follows with an account of Cilly's death. Not long after, she wrote, three men from the Gestapo appeared at Villa Hirsch and ordered her to go with them. Cilly asked if she could collect her coat from upstairs, while her deaf husband sat rocking in his chair, smiling and unaware. She resisted arrest by jumping from the bedroom balcony, and died the following day.

You can't choose what happens to you; you can only choose how you respond. Cäcilie Hirsch chose to resist. She refused to accept or to comply.

I could finish my story of Cilly's resistance here. I first read this somewhat romanticised account of great-grandmother Cilly's life and death many years ago, as a young teenager. I'm not sure whether at that time I fully understood the degree of connection I had with Cilly, just that we were related. Lilli Palmer's account of her interactions with Hollywood celebrities was probably the focus of my interest at that time, being a typical child of the 1970s. I knew that, unlike my Derbyshire-born mum, my dad had started life in Germany, but he was English now, wasn't he? As I said, we had learnt about the Second World War in history classes at school. It was the past, done and dusted.

However, half a century later, I feel less and less sure of who I am, of what made me this person. It is while researching my father's family history that I discover another account of Cilly's acts of resistance. Dr Schier, the sociologist and social psychologist who gave us tea on our visit to Munich in 2014, covered the same attempt to save the Hirschs, including Cilly's death, in her monograph about my grandfather Richard Landauer's publishing business *Delphin-Verlag: The Elimination of a Jewish Publisher*. Yet there are critical differences in these two accounts. A contemporary witness reported to Dr Schier that in November 1938, two months after my grandparents Richard and Edith Landauer had fled to London with their children, Edith had returned to Landshut to persuade her parents to emigrate and join them. On the night of the *Reichskristallnacht*, 9–10 November 1938, Dr Schier was told, Edith was a witness when Adolf was arrested and when Cilly, to avoid being apprehended, died by suicide after throwing herself from the balcony of a top storey window. Edith witnessed hordes of SA members trashing the villa. She was herself imprisoned but released some days later. After returning to London, she found out that her father Adolf had been temporarily released because of his old age, but that he had been incarcerated again shortly thereafter.

Dr Schier wrote:

There had been a notice of death from some concentration camp, the name of which had escaped the lady informant.

I wonder if this source was Erika Stadler, Eva's loyal friend from their teenage years. When Dr Schier was researching for her monograph, Erika Stadler was elderly and failing in health, but in those wartime years she would surely have been alert to any news of the fate of her best friend Eva Landauer's family.

I assume that Lilli, the narrator of her autobiography, was present when her aunt Cilly visited her mother in London, and Dr Schier writes that she took her facts from contemporary witnesses in Landshut. But Cilly died in October 1941, not in 1938. These different versions of the same event, with their different dates for the main events, must either have been mis-remembered or embellished. Or is it just possible that both could be true, that Cilly came to London to visit her sister, Rose, in 1938, and that her daughter, Edith, then visited Cilly in Germany in 1941? Is it credible that, in 1941, Edith had been allowed to leave London, travel to Landshut, and then return safely to London? I don't think so. I doubt whether it was possible for civilians to travel between countries at war.

If, however, she had indeed witnessed the death of her mother only a few years after they had left them behind in Landshut, this trauma would have had a huge impact on her and on the rest of the Landauer family. They had been living so closely with the Hirschs, who had given them both refuge and livelihood in those darkening years from 1933 onwards. And if this is a false account, I wonder whether Edith would have known about the fate of her parents before her own death in 1942. Was personal mail sent through the Red Cross reliable enough to allow for the flow of such information? Did personal international telegrams get through between countries at war? This seems unlikely. I assume the remaining Landauer family in Fitzroy Square only found out about the fate of Adolf and Cilly after the war had ended, by which time Edith herself was dead.

I'm immersing myself in trying to imagine thoughts and feelings. If Edith and her family knew about Cilly's tragedy, they could have experienced intense survivors' guilt, on top of their distress at the manner of her death, and their grief for a much-loved mother and grandmother. It is now recognised that 'survivor's guilt', first described after the Holocaust, is a possible symptom of post-traumatic stress disorder. A person's feelings of guilt and shame can be overwhelming, destroying their mental health and wellbeing – shame that they survived when loved ones didn't, guilt that they didn't do more to save others. I remember my childhood discussions with my father, and my feelings of inheriting these emotions: shame is about who you are; guilt is about what you did.

Both accounts, Lilli's and Dr Schier's, are reported to come from contemporary witnesses. And yet cognitive psychology research shows that eyewitness testimony can be malleable and flawed. There are many factors that affect how an event is laid down in a bystander's memory, and how it is recalled later. Anxiety and stress, threats to life, and the constructionist, sense-making nature of memory all have an impact on accuracy. Any of these aspects may have had an impact on the Landshut witness's account. In particular, Lilli Palmer's account is written in a memoir designed as entertainment; it may have been misremembered or tweaked. Then there is the Chinese whisper effect; stories are changed or embellished every time they are passed on to another, until the final tale may have little in common with the original event.

Then I find still another version of Cilly's death, in the booklet produced by the *Stolpersteine* association of Landshut, which Hans so kindly translated for me. When *Stolpersteine*, 'stumbling stones', were laid for Adolf and Cäcilie Hirsch, this booklet was produced to tell their story. This is how it goes: towards the end of October in 1941, Cäcilie and Adolf were disturbed at Villa Hirsch, the beautiful home they had created little more than a decade earlier, by a Gestapo raid. The Hirschs had been denounced for allegedly having stashed away sizeable amounts of money in their house on *Brühfeldweg*, triggering the Gestapo search. Nazis had made possession of cash illegal for Jews, so they were no longer allowed to hold any currency. During this house search, Cilly fell from the balcony to the ground below.

No agency is specified in this account, so it is difficult to visualise the scene. What is the reader supposed to think – that there was a struggle during which Cilly fell? Or that she was trying to escape? It surely seems more likely that this was a suicide attempt, as she knew what would await her as a concentration camp internee. She had, after all, been involved for some years with those who'd been interned – relatives, friends or strangers. She must have known at least something of the harsh conditions there, although the full horror of torture, starvation and mass murder was only revealed when the liberating troops arrived a few years later. Many Germans took their own lives in these years rather than be arrested by the Nazis.

Cilly was in a serious condition, but still alive after her fall. She must have been in great pain from her injuries. She was taken to the local hospital, where further insult awaited her. The wife of a member of the SA, also a patient in the hospital, ordered the staff to take Frau Hirsch's bed out of the room, as she would not permit a Jew to be in the same room. From this dry account, I have a vivid scene playing in my mind: *'Get her out!' Cilly's bed was placed in a corridor, where she died the next day, on 30 October, 1941.*

To set this in context, the Hirschs' business, their department store, had been confiscated two years previously, on 18 November, 1939. The Hirschs would have had no income since that date, the proceeds of the 'sale' being held in a blocked account. It is very unlikely that they had enough money to live on at this time, let alone any to hoard.

Their home, Villa Hirsch, had been forcibly sold in February 1941, with an agreement that the seller could continue to use living quarters in the house, probably a small part of the whole, until December 1942. However, Cilly had died in October 1941, and on 1 June, 1942, Adolf was transported to a Jewish 'old age home' (*Altersheim*) in Regensburg. All thirty-nine elderly inhabitants were then cleared out by the Gestapo on 23 September and deported via Nuremberg to the Theresienstadt ghetto. A year later, on 22 September 1943, Adolf died, either murdered or a victim of the harsh conditions.

Adolf was seventy-five when he died; Cilly was sixty-five at her death. They should have been retired, enjoying some leisure and watching their grandchildren grow up. Their fellow townspeople should have been helping to care for them in their old age, considering what generous benefactors the Hirschs had been for Landshut, through their deeds and donations, as business-owners and employers.

Instead, an anonymous local had denounced them, and no one had protected them in their time of need. I haven't been told whether anyone in Landshut today knows who the betrayer was. It would serve no purpose for me to try to find out.

And how much did the Landauer family, now safe in London, know of the tragedies happening to those left behind? The questions of who knew what, when and how, eighty years ago are not possible to answer now, but as a psychologist, I am interested in reflecting on the nature of narrative. Humans are story makers, and story recorders, from the earliest cave paintings that told the beholders about the animal world around them. As a thought experiment, one can imagine a period of time as a flat, white sheet, with all its main events spread out as dots over the page. To tell a story coherently, the narrator picks their way from dot to dot, filling in any gaps and skipping over dots where inconsistencies obtrude, to give meaning and flow to the story arc. A 'thin' narrative does not feel satisfying for the storyteller or for the listener, so it is 'thickened' with extra detail – taken from memory or from imagination, from the senses or from emotions. We all do it when relating an event. I am doing it now, consciously and unconsciously, as I try to wrestle my family's story into a shape that will make sense to a reader – and that will help me to forge my identity.

'Get her out!'

The wife of the Nazi storm trooper screamed at the orderlies wheeling my great grandmother's bed into the hospital ward.

'Not in here! I will not share this room with a dirty Jew. I will report you; you will lose your job.'

There was no point in resisting. They pushed the bed back out into the corridor, where, alone and in great pain, Cäcilie Hirsch died the next day, on October 30 1941.

I keep repeating my imagined story of Cilly's death to myself, trying to force into my consciousness the real horror of those events, to recognise the full import. My mind goes back to the civic reception in Landshut, where in the public eye and in the company of our hosts the local dignitaries, I had read the inscription on Cilly's *Stolperstein*:

Here lived Cäcilie Hirsch nee Lissman born 1876 humiliated / disenfranchised fled into death 30.10.1941.

In that exposed moment, I had to cover up my feeling of shock, of distress over the dreadful end for this much-loved woman. I was being called on to lead the laying of flowers, to pose for press photographs – photos that would appear in the *Landshuter Zeitung,* the same journal that, some eighty years earlier, had celebrated the Aryan takeover of the Hirsches' *Hermann Tietz Nachfolger* department store as a symbolic act, signifying that the Landshut economy was free of Jews.

Now as I write this account, I can really study those inscribed words and allow their full meaning into my heart. I remember seeing grainy footage of Jewish men and women, kneeling in their hats and overcoats on cold pavements, forced to scrub the hard surfaces with brushes dipped in acid in front of jeering onlookers. Humiliation indeed. Had anything like that been demanded of Adolf and Cilly? I think of the archivist's gift of the set of photographs chronicling the construction of Villa Hirsch, and look again at the contemporary photograph of *Kaufhaus Tietz,* magnificent buildings that were taken from the Hirsches in an act of legalised theft. Disenfranchised indeed. No wonder Cilly fled into death.

In piecing together what really happened to my great-grandparents, I can recognise many of the event's 'dots', but in the versions I have found, they have been joined up into slightly different stories. Perhaps there may be even more accounts of the Hirschs' last years, if I were to continue to search. (This is why researchers often attempt to triangulate evidence – to reach the closest approximation to truth by measuring in as many ways as possible.)

My purpose in retelling Cilly's story is to honour the quiet resistance of my great-grandmother, Cäcilie Hirsch. Perhaps, though, I am resisting something too. I am not allowing myself to truly feel the terror and pain of Cilly's story, to face the emotional turmoil, instead retreating into an academic reflection on memory and truth – a coping mechanism. But the real import of what happened to the Hirschs doesn't change.

As is recorded on their *Stolpersteine*, Adolf and Cilly were murdered, disenfranchised, humiliated, and fled into death. Still today, this matters to the people of Landshut, and it matters to our family.

Resistance has many forms. Some serve us better than others. I can learn from her example, as I think her daughter Edith and, in turn, my father Robert did. Caring for others means looking for the best in them, and then gently supporting them or sensitively challenging them to grow despite whatever stumbling stones lie in their way. To maintain decency in one's behaviour is the most powerful resistance to evil. It means going high when others go low, as Michelle Obama said. I need to turn this same appreciation back onto myself whenever anxiety or self-doubt threaten to overwhelm my resilience. I must remind myself of my father's cheerful optimism, my grandfather's art for the masses, my grandmother's warm social competence, my great-grandmother's parcels for internees. I have this precious inheritance from my progenitors. My previous coping mechanism was to imagine what was the worst thing that could possibly happen, in order that I couldn't be ambushed by it. Now I remember that whatever you focus on grows. Instead I will copy out some of my father's joyful comments on life and tape them up around me. I add the names and dates of my great-grandparents and grandparents to my perpetual calendar, and lay by some special candles.

29

FINDING EDITH'S GRAVE; LONDON, 2017

There is another Landauer family history discovery in 2017; we find our grandmother Edith's grave in St Marylebone Cemetery (renamed East Finchley Cemetery in the 1990s). We had made an unsuccessful attempt previously, but now with better information from the cemetery's keeper, my sister Reni has tracked it down. A broken concrete rim surrounds the grave. It looks neglected, with a few weeds growing over the concrete paving. There is a rain-stained concrete headstone with inset metal lettering, and none of this looks beautiful or inspiring. But then we read the faded text:

EDITH LANDAUER
BORN 14 JANUARY 1900
DIED 19 DECEMBER 1942
I WAS NOT BORN TO SHARE
MEN'S HATRED BUT THEIR LOVE
AND HER HUSBAND
DR RICHARD LANDAUER
BORN 13 2 1882
DIED 7 8 1960

The quotation is from the third of Sophocles' Theban plays, *Antigone*. It states Antigone's rationale for burying her brother, whom she loved, in defiance of King Creon's martial law. To honour this love is, she says, her nature. The words are a fitting memorial for Edith, whose nature was also summed up by 'love not hatred'.

Edith's gravestone

Richard returned to Bavaria in 1954, to Feldafing where he and Edith had married. Despite being so much older than his wife, he had gone on living for eighteen years after her death. He must have missed her every day until his ashes could finally be buried with her.

I studied Jean Anouilh's version of *Antigone* at school. I shall read it again with a deeper connection to the woman at its heart.

Ever since my infant facility with the Times newspaper was shown off to prospective kindergarten parents in Nairobi, reading has been my go-to cure for every dis-ease. If I am bored or sad, tired or lonely, I find a book to read. When I need to find out about something, I look up written information. Through reading memoirs or fiction, I learn about people and places. I recently found some *Happy Venture* and *Janet and*

John reading books in a charity shop, and just the sight of the pastel-coloured frame around each page of text triggered such a jolt of happiness; I remember reading these books with Mrs Epsom at nursery school. The body remembers joy as well as trauma, it seems.

My reading book

Claire Tomalin describes her dependence on reading in *A Life of My Own*:

> ... being moved about so much, unable to keep friendships going and obliged to start afresh repeatedly, encouraged me to live mostly in books: portable companions, reliable, constant.

This matches my own experience. Throughout my peripatetic childhood and ever since, reading has been a daily necessity. How could I not be drawn towards a book titled *The Reader*? The author, Bernhard Schlink, was a professor in the philosophy of law, and a judge, so it is not surprising that the story centres around punishment and restitution, guilt and shame, secrets and disclosures. I think Robert might have appreciated this complex, multilayered book. At the heart of it is, I believe, the conflict felt by post-war Germans – the natural love and respect felt for one's parents and elders which vies with revulsion and shame for the war crimes they were party to. Another motif is reading. Here, a lack of reading is a metaphor for moral blindness, and education is linked with redemption.

The book spoke to me, even before I was catapulted into my search for my roots, and perhaps it laid the groundwork for my openness to modern Germany. After recognition of trauma, the next step in the healing process is to make reparation, and serendipitously my journey of discovery into my family's past, partly underpinned by books like *The Reader*, seems to have coincided with this stage in Germany's national psyche. *The Reader* gives a cathartic voice to a deep national pain – trauma – and it feels appropriate to re-read it as I explore the repercussions of the Holocaust for my family.

Following the *Stolpersteine* ceremony for the Landauer family in Landshut, we decide to press ahead with applying for dual German citizenship. Under German law, victims of Nazi persecution and their descendants are entitled to reclaim the nationality that was forcibly removed under National Socialism between 30 January 1933 and 8 May 1945 'due to persecution on political, racial or religious grounds'. This certainly applied to the Landauers. Racially Jewish, Robert and his siblings had been deprived of their German nationality and had taken up British citizenship as soon as they could, anglicising their names.

We have to gather so many documents to support our application! – marriage certificates for our grandparents, parents and ourselves, birth certificates for our father, ourselves and our children, our father's British naturalisation certificate ... To complicate matters, those of the family living in England have to apply to the German Embassy in London, whilst we Scots are dealt with by the German Consulate in Edinburgh, each of us having to use the same pack of German documents. Fortunately, we are allowed to quote each other's case numbers and be treated as a family group which speeds up the process a little. We get ourselves organised. It is possible to apply simultaneously for German passports. I decide to wait until I've improved my German language skills before taking that step, imagining the flood of speech that might ensue at the sight of a German passport. I realise I am not – yet! – up to responding.

'We are pleased to accord you citizenship of Germany, with all the rights and responsibilities pertaining therewith, restoring the status which was stolen from your father's family.'

I have mixed emotions as we receive our green *Einbürgerungsurkunden* (certificates of naturalisation), dated 16/03/2017, in a small ceremony – our two sons and I in Edinburgh, our daughter, my siblings and nephews in London. What would Robert have thought? He had been so proud to receive his British naturalisation to replace his confiscated German one. But I think he would have understood and sympathised. He was an ardent internationalist and pacifist. Although the economy was a major reason for the UK to join the European Economic Community in 1973, our generation values the UK's subsequent European Union membership as much for its enlightened social legislation and peacekeeping role as for commercial reasons. Robert would surely have supported these aims wholeheartedly. Along with our German citizenship, we have regained our membership of the European Union, which we lost in 2016's Brexit, and we feel safer for it.

It is my wish to be, firstly, a citizen of a small independent country, an outward-looking Scotland that leans towards social justice; secondly, a European with mutual opportunities for travel, study and commerce with our close neighbours; and thirdly, a member of the United Nations, levelling injustice and working towards global peace. I step up my German lessons through a phone app and over Zoom with a Swiss friend: '*Entschuldigen Sie bitte, wo ist der Bahnhof?*' (Excuse me please, where is the station?) I am determined to achieve a level such that if I am ever to present a German passport, I won't be totally lost when I am addressed in that tongue.

The next generation also have an interest in their German inheritance. They are keen to accompany me on visits to Bavaria, and at Christmas they bake *Elisenkuchen*, spiced gingerbread, lit up by their traditional *Herrnhuter Sterne,* those glowing, star-shaped lanterns.

'I was not born to share men's hatred but their love.' My green *Einbürgerungsurkunde* is the loudest statement I can make of the failure of fascism and hatred, and of the triumph of love.

30

REICHSPOGROMNACHT; LANDSHUT, 2018

Richard, Edith and the children arrived in London on 29 September, 1938. Only a few weeks later, on *Kristallnacht,* the 'Night of Broken Glass', the SA and members of the public attacked Jews, Jewish property and synagogues. Broken glass littered the streets as men attacked buildings with sledgehammers. Many Jewish men were arrested and taken to concentration camps. Some were released later, for a while at least. Several died by suicide, foreseeing all too clearly their bleak future in their homeland.

Also known as *Novemberpogrome* or *Reichspogromnacht,* these events were widely reported by foreign journalists working in Germany, and the Landauers must have been so anxious for Adolf and Cilly left behind in Landshut. The London Times reported:

> No foreign propagandist bent upon blackening Germany before the world could outdo the tale of burnings and beatings, of blackguardly assaults on defenceless and innocent people, which disgraced that country yesterday (11/11/1938).

Landshut is planning a full Memorial Day on the eightieth anniversary, and our family feels honoured to be invited to attend. The main event of the evening is a speech by Dr Moritz Fischer, a historian and a former student of the school Stefan and Robert attended, Hans-Carossa Gymnasium. I am asked to give a brief address too, and we are promised further speeches and klezmer music. In the early part of the evening, some youth groups plan a memorial walk from the *Heilig Geist Kirche* (Holy Ghost Church) to the *Dreifaltigkeitsplatz*, stopping at each set of *Stolpersteine* and reading aloud the biographies of the Jewish citizens who had lived there. We are invited to take part in that too.

The newspaper article in the *Landshuter Zeitung* publicising the event is headed: 'The End of Jewish Life – 80 Years Later', and it mentions the current increase in anti-Semitism, and the need to resist the far right. The article quotes Max Mannheimer:

> You are not responsible for what happened, but you are responsible for making sure that it does not happen again.

We make plans to meet up with Konrad, the chairperson of the *Landshuter Stolpersteine Verein*, and with Johanna's family, and to visit Villa Hirsch. Jan, Angelika's son from her first marriage, who will be visiting from Bratislava, emails me Angelika's hospitable invitation to visit Villa Hirsch. Again, we are a large family party, accommodated variously between hotel and self-catering accommodation. This time there are twelve of us.

In the event, I find the *Reichspogromnacht* procession a disconcerting affair, as the young students have provided us with an Israeli flag to walk behind. The difference between ethnic Jewishness and the political state of Israel is important, in my view. I ask myself whether Israel's encroachment on the state of Palestine goes past self-defence and amounts to a war crime. It seems to me extraordinary that a race who have suffered so much can inflict similar pain on another people, denying them statehood. In the post-war years, Hannah Arendt, best known for her description of the 'banality of evil' at Eichmann's trial, had envisioned a bi-national Arab–Jewish state of equals. She distinguished between Jewishness, an inescapable and existential given, and Judaism, a voluntarily chosen system of beliefs, and accepted the first whilst rejecting the second, in her private capacity. Like Baddiel half a century later, Arendt chose the status of 'conscious pariah' in her awareness of her Jewishness, working for 'an admission of Jews as Jews to the ranks of humanity'. Stoppard made a similar plea in *Leopoldstadt*. In another of life's strange coincidences, I learn that, from 1946, Hannah Arendt had been an editor at Schocken Books, the New York publishing company of Ted Schocken, the husband of Robert's cousin Dora. Had Dora given Arendt the same warm hospitality that Mark and I had appreciated as teenagers in the 1960s?

Because I can't understand the German of the speeches made for each *Stolpersteine* family, I have too much time for such musings, from weighty to trivial, as we progress through the city, each holding a lit candle in a paper collar. It suddenly strikes me that, on this occasion, German is not being translated into English for our ease of comprehension, as on our previous visits. This ceremony was not organised for us, the foreign descendants of Landshut's Holocaust victims. It is for their own townspeople. It is important for them to remember.

At the following *Reichspogromnacht* memorial event in the packed hall of the *Redoutenshaal Bernlochner*, Dr Moritz Fischer speaks in detail about the general situation during *Reichspogromnacht*, and I buy a copy of his newly published book, *Forced Sterilisation and 'Euthanasia' in Landshut*. From it I learnt that a hundred and eighteen men, women and children from the Landshut city and county were 'euthanised' – murdered – and over four hundred and thirty-nine were forcibly sterilised. This is such sombre information. In my own speech, which is repeated in German by my son, Eric, and which we had prepared weeks beforehand, I speak of those lighter moments the Landauer family had experienced at Villa Hirsch. I finish by quoting Edith's gravestone: 'I was not born to share men's hatred but their love'.

There is warm applause, but nevertheless I feel I have misjudged the tone of the occasion; I am glossing over the black shame and deep pain. Perhaps, however, the citizens who turned out in force on a dark November evening need some respite after the harrowing first speech. Certainly the beautiful and haunting Yiddish music that concludes the evening is very welcome, expressing emotion better than any words.

The following day, we make our way back to Villa Hirsch to once more enjoy the hospitality of Angelika and Manfred. On my request, Angelika's son, Jan, takes me round the side of the villa to visit Cilly's summer house.

'I would so like to buy this, to use as a summer cabin,' I say.

'I am so sorry – the land it stands on has already been sold. It's earmarked for development. They have met with some problem with laying the utilities under the ground; this has delayed progress. Otherwise, it would already have been completed.'

I think Angelika had tried to tell me this before, but neither of us had language skills good enough for exchanging complex information, and perhaps that was why she engaged her son, whose English is faultless, to meet with me. In any case – and to come back down to earth – property prices in that part of Germany are so astronomical that I would need a lottery win to afford it (having first bought a ticket ...).

On the last day of our visit, I throw a party for all the many friends we have made in Landshut. In our self-catering apartment, I prepare a giant pasta dish, and borrow extra crockery from the landlord, who is happy to join us. It feels like a fitting end to our third visit to Landshut. Perhaps on my next trip, I can take them this book.

Mutual aid and social connectedness are the principles on which traditional Orkney society is organised. Neighbours give each other their excess produce in times of plenty, and step in to offer skills and labour at times of stress. Shopping – 'getting the messages' – takes for ever as conversations have to be played out in full. It puzzled me once in our local shop when the person serving busied herself elsewhere, ignoring me waiting at the till. When she came over eventually, after the other customer who had been talking to me had left the shop, she said,

'I could see you were wi' owl' Mildred and I ken she likes to spik to someone, being on her own noo ... '

The other day the stone wall above our kitchen window was leaking in a driving easterly rainstorm. I texted a neighbour, who is also a builder by trade, and who keeps us in mackerel fillets from his fishing trips in the summer. He came round first thing the next morning, with two others, father and son, and between them they have come up with a solution. I had just finished my annual marmalade production, and happily shared it among them.

Now I can recognise when I have a need, and ask for help. I know where I come from, and I know where I am. I have not been abandoned; I am held in a network of mutual support. On my journey of discovering who my father's family were, I have learnt of many instances of altruistic goodness, even throughout the evil times of the Holocaust, and I believe we are drawn to positive models. Cilly's food parcels for concentration camp detainees, Richard's 'little books' for the less well-off, Robert's work in the Kikuyu refugee camp, Margaret's interest in each of her Asian pupils – these are my inspirations when I speak at Holocaust Day. And I have met with so many kind souls on my journey of discovery: people who have put themselves out to help me with their research and translation skills, their hospitality and warm interest.

My childhood, with its frequent changes of home, school and friends, culminating in residential education from the age of twelve, was a disrupted one. I learnt to hide from my emotions in books, and to care for others rather than myself. Finding out about my father's family history and wanting to record it for others has forced me to look into myself for perhaps the first time. I have come to realise that telling the Landauers' story cannot be an academic exercise, at arms' length; they are part of me and I of them. Their story is also mine.

In contemporary therapy we are exhorted to parent ourselves: to look at our own failings with kindness and forgiveness, as we would those of our child. Perhaps I am also learning to parent my parents, as I discover more about their backgrounds and early lives. Their childhoods had been forced into strange shapes by a cataclysmic world war; so indeed had their own parents' lives during a previous world war. Nevertheless, Robert and Margaret came of age with hope and passion in their hearts, and made for themselves a different way to live. I am beginning to understand that the people they were, the choices they made, were the consequence of all that had gone before in their lives. They didn't consciously plan that I should have such a dislocated childhood. Like any good-enough parents, they did their best in the situations in which they found themselves. I realise I am beginning to heal. I don't feel so lost any more.

Since my first chance meeting with Hans in 2014, I now have a far clearer understanding of the stumbling stones that have littered my path through life and, more importantly, the strengths I have inherited to overcome them. I can now echo: 'I was not born to share men's hatred but their love'.

31

HOLOCAUST DAY; KIRKWALL, 2020

There were 'so very few' Landauers left, my father had said in his letter announcing my brother's birth ... Holocaust Day falls on my birthday, and just when I am immersing myself in the Holocaust's repercussions for my father's family, I accept an invitation to speak at Orkney's first Holocaust Day event. The year is 2020, the seventy-fifth anniversary of the liberation of Auschwitz–Birkenau, the largest Nazi death camp. It is publicised as a remembrance event for not only the six million Jews murdered during the Holocaust, alongside the millions of other people killed under Nazi persecution, but also subsequent genocides in Cambodia, Rwanda, Bosnia and Darfur. I am relieved that the organisers are giving recognition to the fact that mass murder is still being committed. We cannot let down our guard against homicidal dictators and fascist regimes.

The vigil is held after dark, on the steps of Kirkwall's St Magnus Cathedral. We are asked to bring a lighted candle in a jar, and local musicians play Yiddish music. It is very cold, and the wind whips away our voices, despite the microphone passed to each speaker. My candle holder is blown over, and the shattered glass on the paving stones reminds me poignantly of *Kristallnacht*.

Orkney played a major part in both world wars, because of its natural harbour, Scapa Flow, and its strategic position at the far north of the British mainland. Alongside Neolithic sites of World Heritage status, there are still remnants of twentieth century wartime: the German fleet lying under the waters of Scapa Flow, scuppered in 1919; the gun emplacements, Churchill Barriers and Italian Chapel of the Second World War.

The Orkney archipelago has a strong sense of connection to the outer world, despite its small population of around twenty-two thousand. Orcadians have long been travellers and seafarers, well respected for their navigation and survival skills. Orkney is twinned with the region of Hordaland in West Norway, home of their Viking ancestors. The Italian prisoners of war who built a chapel out of Nissen huts are still remembered and revered through a friendship agreement between our local councils. Altogether it feels fitting that we should honour Holocaust Day in this outward-looking island community.

Kirkwall's Holocaust Day takes place forty years after we first came to live in Orkney. We had intended to stay only a year or so. Travelling was what we had both known all our lives.

But somehow, this feels like home – and the right place to have children; they can be held in a community, go through school with the same cohort, share a childhood, be Orcadian. They will belong. Throughout my first pregnancy, I play Orcadian records to the bump, hoping that the beautiful, lilting Orkney accent and swinging fiddle tunes will set a baseline of home and stability, of lifelong social connection.

My desire to root my children in the culture of their home environment is borne out by what I learn about Kropotkin's theory of evolution. Pyotr Kropotkin, Russian naturalist and anarchist, was born in 1841, and he built on Charles Darwin's work. Each developed a different theory of evolution, but Kropotkin fell out of favour in the Soviet years because of his political views, so the Western world only learnt of his scientific research in the 1950s, decades after his death. Darwin theorised that the race goes to the fittest, that evolution is a matter of competition where the weakest goes to the wall. This fitted the mood of the industrialised and hierarchical society of its time; if a person was defeated by harsh circumstances, it was because they were weaker, and the human race needed only its strongest to survive and breed. Kropotkin, however, had come to a different conclusion through his study of species. His research showed that those who form strong cohesive social groups have the best chances of survival. In his 1902 book *Mutual Aid: a Factor of Evolution* he claims that sociability and cooperation, altruism and reciprocity contribute to survival, and hence to the evolution of species. I could see this philosophy lived out every day in the Orkney way of life, and I wanted our children to grow up in this cultural environment.

I find Kropotkin's notion of 'mutual aid' an attractive philosophy, and I learnt about it at a time when I was developing my skills in Video Interaction Guidance (VIG) and its offshoot Video Enhanced Reflective Practice (VERP). VIG is a therapeutic intervention that uses microanalysis of video to support social connections between people – parent and child, teacher and pupil, doctor and patient – and VERP uses the same method to support professional development. The programme is based on the findings of Professor Colwyn Trevarthen and colleagues, whose work on the earliest interactions between infant and mother showed that babies are born with innate social communication skills. Even premature babies vocalise in a turn-taking pattern with an adult, and newborn infants are programmed to tune into faces, imitating tongue protrusion and finger display shortly after birth. We come into the world primed to be social beings and communicators.

Learning, according to Russian psychologist Lev Vygotsky, takes place through social interactions with a more skilled other, for example a parent or teacher. He describes a 'zone of proximal development' where all teaching and learning take place. At one end of this continuum, a child can only perform a skill with maximum support, and at the other, can perform entirely independently. Psychologist Jerome Bruner used an image of scaffolding to describe the process between these extremes, whereby the child is sensitively supported as they take steps towards competence. The scaffolding is removed when all is going well and instantly replaced whenever there's a wobble.

The VIG and VERP interventions use these insights to help people see those tiny moments when what they are doing in an interaction, even if that isn't their typical behaviour, is having a positive impact. The therapist, or 'guider', takes a short video of an everyday communication event, no more than a few minutes, then microanalyses and edits this, making clips of micro-moments of 'what works'. Each clip is only a few seconds long. Together, guider and client view, re-view and reflect on these clips, discussing ways to build such successful interactions more frequently into daily life. Because this way of acting is already in the client's behavioural repertoire, even if they hadn't been conscious of it, they find it easy to do more of it, and their confidence rockets. A father may see that his baby's eyes follow him across the room, and that his wave of farewell is mirrored by her tiny hand movement, too fleeting to be perceptible without the video evidence –

'I thought she didn't like me ... '

'And here you can see how important you are to her.'

A teacher is shown a moment where, instead of repeating a question then giving the answer, she waits with an expectant smile, and the shy child who never usually speaks actually volunteers a contribution. A teenage boy can see that when he says 'Yes and ... ' instead of 'No but ... ' the others in his group listen to what he says and then build further on it, instead of shouting him down.

I trained in delivering this intervention when I worked as a support teacher for children with special needs, like Freddy, whose mother had been so anxious about my reaction to working with a German. I went on to build my career around this work, training and supervising others and writing books and articles on the method.

I believe that this urge to connect, to respond to the needs and initiatives of others, is at the heart of humanity. It is finding its deepest expression in the interactions I am experiencing as I discover my German roots, with so many people coming forward to face what had happened in the previous generation, and to offer reparation.

EPILOGUE

THE PRESENT DAY

Just as I am drawing this account to a close, I receive an email from a curator of the Bavarian National Museum in Munich.

He is writing to me as the great-granddaughter of Adolf and Cäcilie Hirsch. Dr Mario Tamme, the Landshut archivist whom we had met at our civic ceremony in 2014, had given him my details.

> We have in our museum a salt vessel (see image) that Adolf Hirsch had to bring to a pawn house in 1939, as all Jews living in Germany at that date had to do. In Munich alone, several tons of silver were amassed and mostly melted down. Before this, individuals, institutions and museums had a chance to buy selected objects. Our museum bought three hundred and twenty-two, of which a hundred and twelve remained after the restitutions of the 1950s and 1960s. We are currently also trying to restitute those to heirs of the last legitimate owners.

Hirsch antique silver salt vessel

The little salt dish was made either by Johann Heinrich Nuss (Frankfurt am Main 1762 – 1793, or by Nicolaus Nuss (Frankfurt am Main, 1764 – 1808). It is fashioned from wrought filigree silver and stands on four legs, with a blue glass insert to protect the precious metal from its corrosive contents. Each leg is decorated with a triangular face-like shape and finishes in a graceful inward curve, to bear the weight of its miniature burden. Between each leg is an oval frame containing a basket of flowers. (We have a similar confit dish, a small and delicate fluted bowl supported by perpendicular dolphins, the icon of *Delphin-Verlag*. This must have been so carefully brought out of Germany by Richard and Edith in 1938, before Nazis forced Jewish people to divest their homes of these precious artefacts.) The pawnbroker gave Adolf Hirsch ten RM for the salt dish – a fraction of its value. In today's prices it might fetch three hundred euros.

Adolf and Cilly have 'so very few' third-generation descendants – Stephen's two children and we three children of Robert – and we discuss the curator's offer. We understand their desire to make restitution, to rid themselves of the taint of artefacts gained through crime, and to return such items to their rightful owners. We want to show our appreciation by honouring their intention, yet how can we share one small salt dish between us?

Another solution occurs to us. When we visited the museum in Landshut, we had been both startled and delighted to find a case dedicated to our great-grandparents, the Hirschs, telling their story through photos and artefacts. We decide to offer them the salt vessel; this is its rightful place. It will bear witness to the terrible stumbling stones my father's family faced. Cilly and Adolf, Richard and Edith, Eva and Stefan, Robert and Margaret – they're in my blood and in my heart. Discovering their story – their grief, their resilience – has helped me to understand mine.

The curator signs off his email with this wish:

> ... hoping to be able to close this sad chapter of our museum history.

It is indeed a sad chapter, and I want this account to make a stance 'against forgetting', as the *Stolpersteine* association of Landshut has named itself.

Family possessions can form stumbling stones, blocking the path to a clear future with these remnants from the past. I have come to understand that I no longer need to cling on to them to give me a sense of belonging. I can give them away; I can pass them on to others. Through making connections with my family's history, I have knitted together the loose ends of the fragmented person I was. I know who I am.

ABOUT THE AUTHOR

Miriam Landor has spent her adult life in Scotland, but grew up travelling the world with her German Jewish father and English mother.

Miriam worked in education as a teacher, lecturer and psychologist, and is married with three adult children. Having previously published professional and academic work, she is now turning to memoir to record her family's history and its impact on subsequent generations.

Website: miriamlandor.scot
Mailing list: miriamlandor.scot/subscribe

ACKNOWLEDGEMENTS

I thank all who have so graciously allowed me to include them in my story: my extended family; friends old and new; and in particular, those in public positions in Bavaria whose kindness and humanity have given me, in addition to information, warm friendship.

I thank all those mentors, advisors and groups who've supported my writing, such as Jenny Alexander, Sara Bailey, Jenny Brown, Stephanie Butland, Stephanie Carty, Catherine Deveney, the NaNas, Pens Around The World, Jean Rafferty, Anna Vaught, and Alison Wearing. Robin Phillips and his team at Author Help have guided my steps towards publication.

Thank you to all the authors whose memoirs and Holocaust accounts are filling several large bookcases.

And I am grateful to Orkney, my home for almost half a century, and to everyone who has joined me for a restorative swim in our sea here whenever I needed to wash away the past.